on track ...
Motörhead

every album, every song

Duncan Harris

sonicbondpublishing.com

Sonicbond Publishing Limited
www.sonicbondpublishing.co.uk
Email: info@sonicbondpublishing.co.uk

First Published in the United Kingdom 2022
First Published in the United States 2022

British Library Cataloguing in Publication Data:
A Catalogue record for this book is available from the British Library

Copyright Duncan Harris 2022

ISBN 978-1-78952-173-3

Typeset in ITC Garamond & ITC Avant Garde
Printed and bound in England

Graphic design and typesetting: Full Moon Media

on track ...
Motörhead

every album, every song

Duncan Harris

sonicbondpublishing.com

For my wonderful Ma, who side-stepped my teenage
rebellion phase by saying 'I rather like Motörhead...'

Acknowledgements

The author thanks the estimable Alan Burridge,
Mick Stevenson, Joel McIver, Mick Wall and the other
chroniclers of Lemmy's life and work.

Special love and thanks to my wife, Sammie,
for her constant love, support and encouragement
and, most of all, for getting me in front of the keyboard.

on track ...

Motörhead

Contents

Author's Note

Motörhead have released a shelf full of official studio and live albums. In addition, there have been a trickle of 'grey area' and bootleg albums that are, at best, only marginally worthwhile and are left to collectors.
This book covers all 22 studio albums and the extra songs recorded by the band throughout their career. In addition, Lemmy's prolific solo appearances will be discussed. The criterion for inclusion of any Lemmy solo work is that it must have a significant vocal from him. This means that, surprisingly, the Michael Monroe/Lemmy co-written song 'Debauchery As A Fine Art'(fabulous title) is excluded as Lemmy only contributes distant backing vocals on the chorus. Appearances where he just played bass, produced or provided backing vocals will not be covered.

In addition, all of Lemmy's extra-curricular lyric-writing work for the likes of Skew Siskin, Doro, Ozzy Osbourne, Lita Ford, Huntress, Girlschool, Meldrum and others is discounted.

Lemmy's film and television career (!), including adverts for AXA Equity & Law, Kit Kat chocolate bars and Kronenbourg 1664 lager and even the Simpsons comic strip that he wrote, are entirely beyond the scope of this book. Just accept that Lemmy couldn't really sit still for long, except when he was playing the fruit machines wherever he was.

Cast of characters

Ian 'Lemmy' Kilmister (born 1945, died 2015)

From the moment Lemmy heard rock and roll, he was lost to music. He was also lost to the power of his libido. Seeing the girls in school clustered around musicians, he acquired a battered Hawaiian guitar and, without knowing how to play a note, he turned up at school with his prize. He was surrounded by his female classmates and Lemmy had found his chosen path. At the same school, he also acquired his nickname, although even at the end of his life, he said he had no real idea why they started calling him Lemmy. Various theories have been put forward (the most common being that he was nicknamed Lemmy during his Hawkwind days when he was constantly trying to cadge money with his oft-repeated phrase 'lemme a fiver'), but he was credited as Ian 'Lemmy' Willis on Sam Gopal's 1969 album *Escalator* before Hawkwind had even formed. In retrospect, it seems obvious that his school friends were all fans of the BBC Radio science fiction serial *Journey Into Space* (1953-1958) and cast the seven-year-old Ian as amiable radio operator Lemuel 'Lemmy' Barnet in their playground games.

When he was 16, he saw the Beatles at the Cavern Club in Liverpool and that settled his desire to be a musician. He learnt how to play the guitar, merely adequately as he himself would admit, and set about pursuing his dream. When he ended up as the bass player in Hawkwind, he found his true musical niche. He played it with an attack and a uniqueness that never emerged from his six-string antics.

He was a man of remarkable and brazen contradictions: the lyrical thrust of his songs is always anti-war, but he collected a vast amount of war memorabilia, particularly items related to the Nazis, and was a renowned reader and authority on all sorts of historical wars, Civil and otherwise.

There's no getting away from the fact that Lemmy wrote some profoundly misogynistic lyrics, and yet he was a huge supporter of women in rock (witness his championing of Girlschool, Doro Pesch and Skew Siskin's Nina C. Alice to name a few) and appeared rather chivalrous in his actions, illustrated in the *Lemmy* movie documentary and on the word of Coleen Nolan following his death, for example. He was a man of paradoxes in a world of hegemony.

Lemmy was already well-known for his use of speed by the time he put together Motörhead, as it was a utilitarian drug that allowed him to stay awake for long periods of time. He had taken it for many years as it had been introduced to him while playing in the Rocking Vicars. His drug use may well have started before that, but it became habitual once he was in a band. He was careful to say, throughout his life, that it suited him, but it wasn't for everybody. After a short series of also-rans, Lemmy joined The Rocking Vicars, the definitive 'huge up North' band (who couldn't get arrested in the South, even though they tried!). When The Rockin' Vickers (a name change forced upon them because the original was too incendiary even for the 1960s) folded, Lemmy moved down to London to try his luck there. He found himself staying in Noel Redding's flat for a time, and inevitably that led to his stint as a roadie (and drugs procurer) for Jimi Hendrix. Lemmy found himself joining (and then writing much of the material for) tabla player Sam Gopal and his debut album *Escalator*. He was in psychedelic blues rockers Opal Butterfly for a short stint but recorded nothing with the band, narrowly missing out on the strangely prophetic 'Groupie Girl' single.

He fell into Hawkwind by accident but immediately made his mark providing the definitive vocals for the hit single 'Silver Machine'.Bass was to be his defining sound and he played it with a rhythmic rumble that was addictive, a sound which he'd honed after years of playing rhythm guitar. He was fired from Hawkwind in 1975 (the culmination of years of lateness and band friction) and he returned to the UK from an American tour and wondered what to do next...

Larry Wallis (born 1949, died 2019)
The very first Motörhead guitarist brought both his own songs and a fiery psychedelic blues style to the original line-up. He had been the second guitarist/vocalist to enlist with underground proto-punk legends Pink Fairies, becoming their chief songwriter and vocalist on the rather more structured and melodic *Kings Of Oblivion* album. He assisted Mick Farren (of 'Lost Johnny' fame) and the Deviants on several albums over the decades. He departed fairly smartly from the Pink Fairies as he didn't want 'to get up and jam for ten minutes', preferring to play songs. Suggesting that he wanted to join a 'two-guitar rock band', he was snapped up for the embryonic Bastard, although that plan subsequently went somewhat awry...

Larry resigned from Motörhead after their debut album was aborted by the record company. Larry continued to play and produce throughout his life, even managing two solo albums in the 2000s, but he never became a household name.

Lucas Fox (born 1955)
Lucas was a young friend of Lemmy's who happened to play drums. His recorded contribution to Motörhead is surprisingly sparse (comprising just one song on the original debut album, *On Parole*, and a couple of bonus tracks on the same remaster). For two decades, Lucas lived and worked in France, promoting French music and acting as technical director for various large events. So it came as a shock to discover that he had reappeared, along with ex-Hawkwind bass player Alan Davey, in the rhythm section for the Paul Rudolph-fronted re-activated Pink Fairies on their 2018 hard rock comeback album *Resident Reptiles*.

'Fast' Eddie Clarke (born 1950, died 2018)
Eddie acquired his nickname early on in his career and it referred to his ability to pick at his tremolo bar quickly during his soloing. Eddie started his professional career with Curtis Knight's band Zeus. He recorded an album with

them in 1974, providing the music to one song. Eddie had given up playing music and, by all accounts, was working on refitting a houseboat when he was invited to join Motörhead. Of course, memory being what it is, both Philthy and Lemmy claim to have found Eddie and introduced him to the band.

Following his early 'retirement'/enforced departure from Motörhead, he found further success with blues/hard rockers Fastway, a band supposed to have included Pete Way (ex-UFO) but, er, didn't. Fastway recorded seven albums in their lifetime and Eddie produced two solo albums before his demise. He made several guest appearances in the 2000s, both on album recordings and live, but the fire of creation largely seemed to lapse once the earliest version of Fastway collapsed.

Phil 'Philthy Animal' Taylor (born 1954, died 2015)

It is no stretch to suggest Philthy had undiagnosed ADHD (Attention Deficit Hyperactivity Disorder), given the somewhat manic way he lived his life. Motörhead were his first real band and he provided the engine that threw them from surprisingly lumpy pub rock to the ferocious speed freak rock and roll band that they will always be remembered as. When Philthy left to join with Brian Robertson in the ill-fated Operator venture, he appeared to be searching for both kudos and recognition as a serious musician. The failure of that project sent him back to Motörhead, but the hiatus had disappointed him and Lemmy said that, from his side, taking Philthy back had been a mistake. After he was fired again in 1992, Phil ducked out of music until the 2000s, when he began jamming and recording with James A Childs (of nearly huge UK band Airbus) in L.A. This set the scene for the recordings to be completed (adding bass and vocals and hammering them into the shape of songs) and then posthumously released under the name Little Villains. So far, two albums have appeared, making the most of the drummer's input, called *Philthy Lies* (2019) and *Taylor Made* (2020). You can probably see what they did there.

Brian 'Robbo' Robertson (born 1956)

Boasting a remarkably strong track record prior to joining Motörhead, Brian was an alumnus of the hugely successful twin-guitar era of Thin Lizzy, joining the band when he was only 18. When Brian was fired from Thin Lizzy, he returned to his own group, Wild Horses. The two albums they released were moderately successful but lacked the spark that had ignited Thin Lizzy in their heyday.

Brian joined Motörhead as a favour to 'some friends' and it should have been regarded as a significant coup obtaining his services. Unfortunately, Brian played and dressed (!)as if he was in a different band. His departure was inevitable.

When Brian was let go from Motörhead, after only 18 months, he took Philthy with him to Operator. They signally failed to attract any attention and the lack of a record deal put paid to their grand ambition. Brian found himself making guest appearances both live and on record for over two decades, but the first new music heard from him was a solo album, *Diamonds and Dirt*, eventually released in 2011.

Phil 'Zoom'/'Wizzo'/'Lord Axesmith' Campbell (born 1961)

Phil Campbell was relatively young when he joined Motörhead, although he had previously been in little known Welsh rockers Persian Risk and he became the de facto mainstay of the band for three decades, writing the majority of the music on the albums when they reverted to their trio line-up in 1996.

When Motörhead disbanded, Phil regrouped and carried on creating music. He has produced a solo album and several band albums under the name Phil Campbell and the Bastard Sons, with his musician progeny. His initial idea, to call this group Phil Campbell's All-Starr Band, foundered on the rocks of irony when people asked what Ringo Starr was doing in the group! Actually, it had been named after the singer the band had recruited, Neil Starr. The potential for confusion was too much, so the new name was hastily inserted onto tour posters and the first studio release from the band.

Michael 'Wurzel' Burston (born 1949, died 2011)

Wurzel was an entire unknown when he auditioned for the second guitarist role in 1983. He had played in nothing more than pub bands, but Lemmy liked what he heard and, more importantly, enjoyed Wurzel's company from their first meeting. Wurzel's background as a soldier appealed to Lemmy immensely. During his tenure in Motörhead, Wurzel did manage to release one solo 12' single, 'Bess', as an adjunct to the soundtrack of the 1987 film *Eat the Rich*, which Motörhead provided. Following his departure, Wurzel virtually retired from music. In 1998 he reportedly produced a limited edition improvised ambient album entitled *Chill Out or Die* (!) but otherwise largely stayed away from music for almost another decade before co-founding and recording with rock/metal band Leader Of Down, who posthumously released their debut album in 2018. Lemmy was obviously saddened by Wurzel's untimely death and frequently referred to him as a close friend, even during Wurzel's wilderness years after he had left Motörhead.

Pete Gill (born 1951)

Pete has a long and distinguished history as a drummer: he was initially one of the two drummers in The Glitter Band (following their split from Gary Glitter) before becoming a founding member of Saxon in 1978 and appearing on their first four landmark albums. He was brought in to Motörhead when Mikkey Dee declined the band's first offer. Pete didn't really live Motörhead's hedonistic lifestyle, preferring, it is said, a cup of tea and an early night in contrast to the rest of the band, and was ousted when Philthy decided to return. Pete went quiet after he was ejected from the group, only performing in local pubs and with cover bands. He did appear on an album by Son Of A Bitch in 1996, but little was to follow because, unfortunately, Pete was forced to retire from drumming due to severe arthritis in his hands, legs and back. Reportedly he had to detox from alcohol in 2004, obviously self-medicating the pain from his chronic disease, and little has been heard of him since.

Mikkey Dee (born 1963)

Micael Kiriakos Delaoglou plays under the stage name Mikkey Dee. A remarkable rock drummer, he has worked with King Diamond and Dokken. Mikkey was asked to join the band before Pete Gill but declined as he felt he wasn't up to the standard they required, which immediately endeared him to Lemmy. Don Dokken's solo career petered out and the band again saw their opportunity to bag a world-class drummer, so they offered the role again and this time, he accepted. After Lemmy's death, he and Phil Campbell jointly stated that Motörhead were over. Mikkey then briefly joined the reactivated Thin Lizzy, but personality clashes led to his swift departure. Instead, Mikkeywas headhunted to join hugely successful German rockers Scorpions, although this was largely for touring commitments until 2022 when they finally released an album of new material.

Joe Petagno (born 1948)

Forever associated with Motörhead, Joe has been a sought-after artist and graphic designer for decades. His ultimate claim to immortality is surely the creation of the iconic Motörhead graphic that adorns their debut album. Oddly, the armoured and tusked pig skull has gone under many names: Snaggletooth (my personal favourite), the War Pig (a blatant lift from Black Sabbath too far), the Iron Boar (Sabbath territory again?), the Bastard or the Little Bastard (Joe's preferred monikers, undoubtedly because of the band's original name). Joe has illustrated many album and single covers and has also produced science fiction book covers as well as other paintings. After apparently falling out with Motörhead's management, Joe ceased to produce cover art for them beyond *Kiss of Death* in 2006.

Introduction

If we moved in next door, your lawn would die!

Motörhead were the greatest rock & roll band ever. Fact. The Rolling Stones may have branded themselves with that coveted accolade, but Motörhead never veered into disco or flirted with reggae and they stayed entirely true to their musical principles. It took some time for Motörhead to win that honour, though. Firstly they had to deal with wayward producers, hostile record companies, more than a couple of false starts and even the ignominy of being proclaimed the Worst Band in the World by the *NME*!

Having been so humiliatingly fired from Hawkwind for, as he put it, 'doing the wrong drugs', Lemmy set about creating Bastard, the ultimate rock 'n' roll band figuring, correctly, that he was unlikely to sack himself from his own band.

Lemmy's initial idea was a four-piece rock and roll band with twin guitarists in the mould of Thin Lizzy. He had struck up a friendship with Lucas Fox and they scouted out possible guitarists, Lemmy deciding that bass playing was where he really belonged. He noted in his autobiography:

I really found myself as an instrumentalist in Hawkwind. Before that, I was just a guitar player who was pretending to be good, when actually I was no good at all. In Hawkwind, I became a good bass player. It was where I learned I was good at something.

Next to join the nascent Bastard was seasoned musician Larry Wallis. The final piece of the quartet was due to be guitarist Luther Grosvenor (aka Ariel Bender), fresh from his time in Mott The Hoople. Had he joined, the name might have changed to the Four L's (Lemmy, Luther, Larry, Lucas), which became the Four Hells and might have been the Four Horsemen thereafter. It was not to be as Luther started his own band, Widowmaker, at precisely the same time as Bastard were looking for that all-important second guitarist. Luther even went so far as to recruit ex-Hawkwind alumnus Huw Lloyd Langton for the supporting guitar slot in Widowmaker, cutting off another option for Bastard. In the mid-1970s, the pool of talent was surprisingly thin.

The Name
First off, the name Bastard was deemed too brazen and confrontational for comfort, band manager Doug Smith (inherited from Hawkwind) pointing out to Lemmy that a vast number of shops would be unlikely to stock anything with that band name and gig posters were likely to be removed immediately.

Accepting the negative advice ('you can't call yourselves Bastard!'), and realising that the quartet would only be a trio, Lemmy had a quick rethink and settled on the name Motörhead. It was, after all, the final song he had written and recorded for Hawkwind, but it also had a huge resonance with him as it was an American slang term for a speed (amphetamine) freak.

The stuttering start of Motörhead (1975-1977)

Taking advantage of his Hawkwind leftovers (he was still signed to a manager, he still, staggeringly, had a recording contract), the band went to Rockfield Studios in Wales in October of 1975 and set about recording with gusto. They had secured, via their United Artists record company, the services of Dave Edmunds as their producer and they were delighted. Edmunds had come up through rock and roll and rockabilly and was a veteran of his own hit singles and producing hits for others. Unfortunately, he found himself in the middle of negotiations to sign with Led Zeppelin's record label Swan Song and didn't have his mind on the job. Concurrently, Lemmy and Larry were engaged in an unlikely duel to see who could stay awake for the longest. Rather predictably, this hamstrung the sessions and very little was completed before Dave Edmunds departed. The staff producer at Rockfield, David 'Fritz' Fryer, was drafted in at short notice to helm the rescheduled sessions, starting in December 1975, and then had to contend with the decision that Lucas Fox wasn't up to the task and the band needed a new drummer. Lemmy almost immediately recruited Philthy (based entirely on Philthy's boast that he was a bloody great drummer) and was floored when Philthy re-recorded the drums for almost the entire album during January and February 1976. This was akin to taking out the load-bearing walls in a house and then rebuilding them from the inside. Philthy was unable to overdub new drums onto every track, however, as he missed the session for 'Lost Johnny' when he was arrested and locked up for being drunk and disorderly. Philthy's reputation for unconstrained 'larking about' started early on.

Once all that had been completed, the album was presented to United Artists and...shoved in the back of a dusty cupboard. The label were reportedly horrified by the lack of commercial prospects from this scuzzy and low rent slice of biker rock and shelved the album indefinitely.

In the meantime, the band struggled to carry on. Larry suggested that they add a second guitarist, as originally intended, and either Philthy or Lemmy came up with 'Fast' Eddie Clarke for the post. Larry, for reasons that remain unclear, decided that he was out of the group after Eddie had auditioned and so the first stable line-up was accidentally created.

By the time Motörhead were a touring proposition, Lemmy had already instigated one of several changes from the norm: in this case, it was placing his microphone at an unusually high position then angling the microphone downwards so he could sing to the rafters of any venue. There were questions about whether he was trying to blot out the audience or if he could play his bass without seeing it, but he always replied that he used the stance purely because he felt it was the most comfortable.

When the reconstituted band reconvened after the *On Parole* debacle, it was simply to tour consistently. A lifeline was offered in the form of a one-off single for the now-legendary and then fashionable, Stiff Records. The band and their management paid for the session and added their first self written song, 'White Line Fever', as the b-side. With the whole band clattering bravely through the unlikely a-side, Lemmy sang the Motown standard 'Leavin' Here' as if he was gargling glass while sitting in a dingy pub in London. It appears that United Artists got wind of the release and, rather than seeing any value in promoting the band, actually stopped the single from being distributed in the UK. Bummed out, as the band later put it, that their recording career hadn't even got off the starting blocks, the band ploughed on with any live work that they could pick up.

Around March 1977, the band were seriously thinking of calling it a day, having had no luck attracting any record company support, so they decided they should record their final gig and asked Ted Carroll if he would be interested, having finally seen the end of their United Artists contract. Ted was eager and the plans were set to record at the Marquee Club in April 1977. A gigantic snag cracked the horizon when the Marquee Club informed the band and management that they required a fee to 'facilitate' the recording. The paltry budget was barely enough for the recording tape and the hire of Eddie's friend, 'Speedy' Keen, to produce it,so the idea, like so many of Motörhead's early plans, collapsed. Instead, Ted suggested they record a single and try to rearrange the live recording for another venue. Ted waved the band off cheerily to Escape Studios in Kent and then followed them down a day later to pay part of the fee for the studio time. He was astounded when Eddie told him they had already put down twelve backing tracks and rough mixes were being produced, remembering that the band had only been there for 24 hours. Ted, not without trepidation at the cost implications, agreed to the completion of the album if they could ensure it was done within another two days, to which the band agreed.

The lack of songwriting in the intervening couple of years is surprising but perhaps not unjustified: the band always felt they were on the verge of splitting up or falling apart and saw no need to create more songs that might be lost to posterity. Aside from re-doing 'White Line Fever', the extra songs recorded at these sessions were cover versions and one trio-written instrumental (they, inevitably, didn't have time to add the vocals).

Immediately upon receiving the tapes, Chiswick Records set about mixing and releasing their debut single: 'Motörhead' (an easy choice given the band's name and the desire to get that name out into the world), backed with their version of the Pink Fairies 'City Kids'. The single charted, albeit stalling at #51, which was enough impetus to get the album finished and issued.

Almost in spite of themselves, the band couldn't help but cause more difficulties by changing management during the run-up to the album release. Doug Smith was ousted and Tony Secunda(of industry heavyweights Wizard Management, who had previously represented the Move, the Moody Blues, Procol Harum and Marc Bolan) was instated and the band looked forward to superior representation and, therefore, a major record deal following their first release. The debut album was more successful than anticipated and it earned them a high enough chart placing that they felt re-invigorated and gave them the impetus to forge on.

Motörhead (Chiswick, August 1977)

Personnel:
Lemmy Kilmister: vocals, bass
Fast Eddie Clarke: guitars
Philthy Animal Taylor: drums
Produced at Escape Studios, Kent in April 1977 by (the aptly named) 'Speedy' Keen.
Highest chart place: UK: 43
Running time (approximate): 32:52

'Motörhead' (Ian Kilmister)

When the title track was initially recorded for the cruelly shelved first album, this ode to amphetamines opened with the sound of throaty motorbike engines revving up. These were from a local Hell's Angels chapter who were quite upset when the record didn't appear for several years. This engine revving is a nice little piece of misdirection by the early band to disguise the lyrics, which aren't about motorcycles so much as they concern the speed-fuelled touring by Hawkwind. Lemmy wrote a scuzzy counterpart to Hawkwind's blatant 'Kings of Speed' song, and used it as the b-side for the last single he would play on for them. Delighting in the fact that this is the only rock and roll song to feature the word 'parallelogram', Lemmy also relished the chance to re-record the song as Motörhead were playing it at a much faster tempo and favoured a far dirtier sound. It all hangs on the initial bass riff and the shouted chorus, but it wouldn't reach its apotheosis until it turned up on *No Sleep 'til Hammersmith* where it finally ends up as the surging embodiment of drug-fuelled abandon it was always intended to be. The band make a pretty good attempt to capture that on *Motörhead,* but the rolling drum introduction doesn't quite capture the sheer pace that they were looking for. Ultimately it is the drumming that, strangely, lets the side down. Philthy is needlessly restrained and loves that breathless tour of his kit so much that he repeats it far too often. There's always the definitive version on *No Sleep 'til Hammersmith* to keep everyone happy, though.

'Vibrator' (Derek Brown/Larry Wallis)

Hardly subtle in its subject matter, this ode to battery-assisted female orgasms at least has a great deal of verve and doesn't take itself too seriously (it's not possible to sing along with 'V-v-v-vibrator' without laughing). Originally this was sung by Larry Wallis for the stillborn debut, where it sounded like a good demo but lacked the polish and sharpness of this re-recording. This was co-written by Larry and band roadie Derek 'Des' Brown while no one was looking. Certainly, no one was much in the mood for writing new songs. With a sped-up rock and roll undercarriage and a sterling main riff, this had potential but, aside from the chorus, this is musically unmemorable. This comically scabrous tune was largely forgotten once it appeared here, disappearing from the setlists almost the moment it had been finally laid to tape.

'Lost Johnny' (Mick Farren/Kilmister)

Although a musical nod back to Lemmy's rock and roll roots, this has Mick Farren writing disquieting words to a spirited bass-heavy tune. Mick throws in a mish-mash of ideas lyrically (werewolves, vampires, crocodiles living in the sewers of New York, characters named Sally and Simon, and mentions of morphine, tuinal and valium) but fails to tie the song together with a single theme or statement. It is very atmospheric lyrically and that can often make up for any shortcomings. Lemmy gives his utmost in the vocals, even dropping in a high-pitched cry of sheer abandon, and the band give this old warhorse of a Hawkwind tune its final epitaph in glorious style, Eddie stylishly adding some lovely parting guitar figures. Deliberately, the band and producer finish this with the old live flourish technique and then head straight into...

'Iron Horse/Born To Lose' (Brown/Guy 'Tramp' Lawrence/Phil Taylor)

After the breezy gallop of the previous songs, it is curious to hear the pace slowed to a gentle canter at this point. However, the rolling groove of the music captures the mood nicely and the verse guitar riff is addictive. In stark contrast, the chorus music is unprepossessing and somewhat forgettable and works in contradiction to the sturdy chorus vocals. The words concern an outlaw motorcycle gang and carry a mythological weight to them that isn't necessarily noticeable on first hearing but start to infect your head once played a few times. The 'Iron Horse' is the motorbike and the 'Born to Lose' axiom is the pessimistic result of their belief that these guys won't last long. The song was brought to the sessions by Philthy and was co-written by him, roadie 'Des' Brown and a Hell's Angel friend of the band ('Tramp'). It pulses along inventively and became an unexpected highlight on *No Sleep 'til Hammersmith*, as it is here, even with the lacklustre chorus tune.

'White Line Fever' (Eddie Clarke/Kilmister/Taylor)

This is a simple but expressive road song which is the first song the band wrote together. Inevitably it concerns touring and live gigs. The white line they are referring to being the one in the middle of the road, as they constantly travel around the country playing every pit, dive and toilet that was around in 1976. The connection with cocaine cannot be ignored either, the feverish abandon brought on by that line of white powder fuelled many a band through many a live appearance and beyond.

Boasting a heavy and crunchy guitar riff, Lemmy's vocals sound like they were recorded in a tin box rather than a studio, but the sheer bravura chutzpah of the band gets them through this brief, almost punk length, debut at songwriting. Barring the clichéd 'live' finale, used to better effect on 'Lost Johnny' earlier, this is a brilliant hint that the band are not entirely reliant on covers (and their own old songs) for their repertoire.

'Keep Us On The Road' (Clarke/Kilmister/Taylor)

Placing two self-written touring songs next to each other is an interesting gambit. This time the lyrical focus is on the dogged persistence of the band to just keep going, given the hardships and setbacks they have already suffered and the transient delights of groupies. The song perhaps shows a lack of variety in subject matter, but it also predicts the majority of Lemmy's life from here on in – touring his arse off throughout the world for decades to come.

Stretching this song out to almost six minutes, the band opt for the slow-burning blues-rock epic rather than speeding up the tempo for a quintessential Motörhead charge. Thrashing about for another fake live ending, the band lack any hint of inventiveness and illustrate, once and for all, that these backing tracks were recorded as if the band were at a gig.

'The Watcher' (Kilmister)

This ancient song, even at the time of this album, was retooled for the umpteenth time to find its final resting place here. When Lemmy first wrote this for Sam Gopal's 1969 album *Escalator*, it was called 'You're Alone Now' and lacked a drummer. Lemmy kept the brooding melody and downbeat outlook but changed everything else when he repurposed the song for Hawkwind in 1972, renaming it 'The Watcher'. Lemmy opted for an ominous warning of the Big Brother state and its blanket CCTV surveillance in his rewritten lyrics, while the dour chords suggested a much darker and more miserable future.

Not handicapped by having to overdub new drum tracks onto already recorded rhythm tracks, Lemmy and Philthy could lock together and tear through this golden oldie with aplomb, intending to race through it as if they were teenagers. Lemmy, in particular, glories in the driving bass he can now equip the song with. The problem is that this song just doesn't suit this rockier approach. All the atmosphere, all the brooding menace that made the Hawkwind version so special, has been lost and only a pale shadow remains. On the verses, Lemmy double-tracks his voice to make it sound robotically inhuman, which fits admirably with the lyrical content, but the intermittent phasing (that whooshing sound) and the inevitable counterfeit 'live' ending, coupled with the psychedelic Hawkwind production tricks, make this final studio version a sad disappointment.

'Train Kept A-Rollin'' (Tiny Bradshaw/Howard Kay/Lois Mann [aka Syd Nathan])

Placing this remarkably tired standard of a song at the end of the album seems flawed at best. Originally recorded in 1951 (Lemmy was only five at the time!), this was a staple of rhythm and blues bands for decades (The Yardbirds, Led Zeppelin and even Aerosmith covered it before Motörhead joined in), and it had undoubtedly reached saturation point by the time Lemmy and crew trawled through their collective memories to find another

21

song for the album. Lemmy provides a strained weather-beaten vocal and the band thrash through the tune, but it's just a little too 'heard-it-all-before' given its prominent position. Bowing out on echo and brio, this is a poor finish to a promising debut. Lyrically it sits in the band's milieu well, predicting songs like 'Locomotive' and 'Ridin' With The Driver', with the train/sex metaphor making its first appearance in the Motörhead oeuvre, but it does sound just a little desperate.

Related recordings

'City Kids' (Duncan Sanderson/Wallis)

This was a relatively recent Pink Fairies song (from 1973) that almost completed the re-recording of the entire first album, although it only managed to sneak out as a b-side. Some spirited playing from all involved, particularly Eddie, again playing on someone else's song, can't disguise the basically ramshackle nature of the tune, although it shines a little brighter than the original. It continues to reference the late 1960s production values with more phasing and echo, and this leaves the listener feeling that this version is actually older than the original. Lemmy's vocals are thoroughly dreadful; it is almost as if he is trying to remember the words while he is slurring his way through them. Part of the problem is that there is no multi-tracking of the vocals, which leaves Lemmy's croak worryingly bare. He does sound like he is enjoying himself, with all his extraneous cackling, but it is nowhere near his finest performance.

'Beer Drinkers and Hell Raisers' (Frank Beard/Billy Gibbons/ Dusty Hill)

This, and the following three songs, eventually saw the light of day some years into the band's success (joining *On Parole* in that regard), although they were recorded at the same sessions as the rest of their self-titled album. This, the title track of the EP, is a very quirky duet between Lemmy and Eddie (who sounds like he's channelling a cut-price Glenn Hughes here) of an ancient ZZ Top song where Eddie takes the high notes as Lemmy can't quite reach those heights without grabbing his bollocks to a painful degree. It doesn't sound much like the original, for what that's worth, but it certainly doesn't bode well for the apparent lack of songwriting going on. Lyrically, of course, it fits Motörhead like a glove. Lemmy may have preferred Jack Daniels and coke, but the band were all drinkers of one sort or another and, more than a decade away, there would be a song called 'Hellraiser' brought into the Motörhead fold.

'On Parole' (Wallis)

Another re-recording, this time of the otherwise missing debut title track. A brazen rock and roll song dressed up with some chunky guitar on the choruses, some treble-y soloing from Eddie (who, again, provides a few backing vocals) and an elongated ending that goes nowhere in the manner of the rest of the album. Chorus-wise, the song seems to owe a debt to Hawkwind's 'Back On The Street' single from 1976, but the lyrics are a little more introspective ('stop me now before I kill myself') and uncomfortable. Lemmy wouldn't cover lyrical territory like this again for some years.

'Instro' (Clarke/Kilmister/Taylor)
The intention was to add vocals to this somewhat barrelling blues-rock backing track but time constraints (as ever) left this as an instrumental. Given that it was only released as part of an EP long after it was recorded, it has, at least, curiosity value and proves to be a nice little showcase for all three musicians. Considering that the band recorded twelve other tracks in this marathon three-day session, it's a miracle that this was committed to tape at all. Although never used as such, this would have made a great intro tape for the band and given a few of the older fans a buzz of secret recognition.

Lemmy remarked in later years that Motörhead would only record an album's worth of material because, as has been seen, previous record companies could capitalise on their success by putting out EPs such as this one. Lemmy also acknowledged that he didn't begrudge this particular EP issue as he was forever grateful to Ted for funding their first released album.

'I'm Your Witchdoctor' (John Mayall)
The original recording of this well-known song, from 1965, was produced by Jimmy Page and featured Eric Clapton. Eddie probably ignored the weight of expectation given that pedigree and treated it like all the other songs here: something that had to be put on tape in double quick time, both literally and figuratively. The band take this at breakneck pace and give a nod to the song's blues origins, but this is another Motörhead mugging of a classic. Given that this was demonstrably Lemmy's band, he allows Eddie to sing surprisingly often in these early years. His vocals are perfectly acceptable (as is this thudding take on the song), but there is very little to distinguish this from other bands of the time except for the phased and distorted late entry of Lemmy's far more distinctive howling cackle. Live set-lists were peppered with hoary old covers like this, but it was a wonder that the band could put together enough music for an hour as a support band, never mind the number of songs needed as a headliner; in one infamous case, Motörhead played their entire set as a headliner in 30 minutes, only to be pushed back on to the stage by the dumbstruck promoter to do the whole thing all over again! Such are the dangers of relying on amphetamines...

After The Debut Album
It is small wonder that these left-overs were dusted off and given a new lease of life after the remarkable success of the *Ace of Spades* album and single in November 1980, but it wasn't the first time that a record label had hit the

button marked 'cash-in'. After the success of *Overkill* and *Bomber* in 1979, United Artists realised they had an entire unreleased Motörhead album in their vaults that wasn't earning its keep and put it out for Christmas 1979, less than two months after the *Bomber* album had cracked the Top 20.

After the undoubted excitement of finally releasing their not-quite debut album and getting some well-deserved recognition, Motörhead went inexplicably dormant for a time, largely touting for gigs and marking time with rehearsing. The big splash of their self-titled album caused no ripples in record company circles and the band found themselves treading water, just as they had a year earlier. It was almost as if the album had never existed. So much so that Lemmy joined the remaining three-quarters of The Damned (Dave Vanian, Captain Sensible, Rat Scabies) as Les Punks for a one-off gig and then guested with The Doomed (again The Damned, this time concerned about any legal action from ex-member Brian James) in 1978 for several gigs and was even reported to have joined the band full-time by one music paper. Talk inevitably turned to the future of the band and, ultimately, the blame was laid at the door of Wizard Management and Motörhead returned to Doug Smith, presumably relying on the old adage 'better the Devil you know.'As it was, Motörhead soon gained an unexpected boost when up and coming record label Bronze (headed by the charismatic Gerry Bron) agreed to a simple 7'single release. The band evidently hadn't learned from their previous experience with the one-off record deal or thought it was worth another chance, but it did result in:

'Louie Louie'(Richard Berry)
Highest chart place: UK: 68
The song itself was written in 1955 and had become a standard rock and roll number within the decade. By the time Motörhead got hold of it, the song had long been over-exposed and overplayed. Frank Zappa had satirised it by having it played live on the Royal Albert Hall pipe organ for the Mothers of Invention album *Uncle Meat* in 1969 and even then, it sounded totally out-of-date.

Motörhead threw a punk-influenced, sped-up arrangement at the song and attacked it with teenage vigour (and the incongruous use of the cowbell!), ending up with a minor charting single, bludgeoning their way, it seemed, to recognition. No one could call this version innovative or even particularly interesting, but it served its purpose well and it prevented the break-up of the band.

Overkill (Bronze, March 1979)

Personnel:
Lemmy Kilmister: vocals, bass
Fast Eddie Clarke: guitars
Philthy Animal Taylor: drums
Produced at Roundhouse and Sound Development Studios, London, December
1978-January 1979 by Jimmy Miller.
Highest chart place: UK: 24
Running time (approximate): 35:15

The 'Louie Louie' single performed well enough in the charts (aided by a
fortuitous *Top Of The Pops* appearance) that Bronze almost immediately
requested an album. Choosing the American Jimmy Miller (famed for his
extraordinary run of albums with the Rolling Stones) as their producer was a
brave and ultimately inspired decision which implied faith in the band that was
only slightly tarnished by the short recording time that Bronze could afford.
Bronze, perhaps coincidentally, also signed Hawkwind and Girlschool to their
label around the same time. Both were to figure in Motörhead's future.

Learning from his time in Hawkwind (where arguments over songwriting
credits have continued to fester almost to this day) and recalling his first
writing and publishing experience with Sam Gopal (although he actually wrote
all the songs, except the cover versions, for the album *Escalator* he credited
half of them to 'Group' to lessen the disparity between the writers and non-
writers in the band) Lemmy instituted a pretty strict policy of equally shared
writing credits within Motörhead for the remainder of the band's career.
There are a few exceptions where Lemmy gains a sole credit as he presented
the songs complete to the band (often because they were written for specific
projects outside of Motörhead), but these are rare.

For practically their entire career, Motörhead wrote their songs in the same
way: they rehearsed a set of riffs which they formed into tunes, usually allowing
the producer to pitch in with their ideas and comments at this early stage, and
then, once they were satisfied, the band would create a master backing track
for each song ready for the words to be written and the vocals and overdubs
(guitar solos, etc.) to be added nearer the end of the recording process. Neither
of the previous albums were achieved this way (as the songs already existed,
sometimes even having multiple earlier recordings to draw on), but this would
become the standard for the rest of their career. It's how Lemmy was able
to create lyrics (and sometimes vocals) for all manner of guest appearances.
Again, it was all down to Lemmy's preference (although many producers find
it the hardest way to work as they often don't have an idea of what the lyrical
direction might do to a song) and, at the time, it was considered an unusual
method of working. Lemmy remarked that he 'couldn't do it any other way'. Try
to imagine listening to the following songs as instrumentals and marvel at the
way Lemmy seems to find the apposite words on almost every occasion.

Lemmy had a remarkable vocabulary and was a literate and intelligent man, he was a voracious reader (mostly on the tour bus as there was nowhere else that he could concentrate), and he wrote some marvellous lyrics. So, it can only be assumed that he meant to recycle himself lyrically when he took lines and phrases from previous lyrics and turned them into new songs. *Overkill* is full of these allusions to future work: 'I got mine', 'live to win', 'stab you in the back' and others pop up with startling regularity.

Early Motörhead, however, is the sound of musical heavyweights battering down your door with the volume turned up to 11 and only a nano-particle of subtlety. This was what they ultimately wanted to convey with their blazing second album. So they named it...

'Overkill' (Clarke/Kilmister/Taylor)

Already reinventing themselves from the borderline pub rock of their (twin) debut(s), this opening salvo sets the agenda for the next 35 years in one breakneck (the story of Philthy taking this literally comes later) rollercoaster. Punk had broken in 1976 and introduced people to amphetamine-fast loud music, but nothing prepared the listening world for the blistering double kick drum stampede that opens this remarkable album. That primal thundering attack is driven by Philthy's psychotic panache. While the three players are credited with writing the song, this is undoubtedly Philthy's moment from the battering beginning through the double breakdowns all the way through to the final end.

'Overkill' isn't so much a song as it is the sound of an earthquake, both literal and metaphorical. The earth certainly moves when the needle hits the groove (or however you play your music), but this single song is rightly acknowledged as the birthplace of both thrash and speed metal, whole new sub-genres of music, which quickly spawned Metallica, Megadeth, Slayer, Anthrax and others. If Motörhead had imploded at the end of this album, they would still be remembered as seminal for this single brutal, inspirational and glorious song. Lemmy puts forward Motörhead's mission statement in the very opening lines of the title track:

Only way to feel the noise is when it's good and loud
So good you can't believe it, screaming with the crowd...

And they didn't deviate for the next 36 years.

Those breakdowns that permeate the song seem beholden to the inspiration of Hawkwind's 'Master Of The Universe', a song which Lemmy greatly enjoyed playing with the band for many years and which he often noted that he wished he had written.

It is astonishing that Motörhead weren't sued a thousand times over for breaking the speakers of their listeners. This was the first single from the forthcoming album and, when played on the radio, the compression and lack of definition in the sound was the result of the flattening of the noise demanded by the restrictions of the radio technology of the period. Once, however, you got the vinyl on your own turntable, it pummelled out of the speakers like a herd of runaway elephants and many systems were undoubtedly blown, especially if you had followed the advice to play it 'good and loud' as the lyrics demanded!

It feels like all the frustration, rage and pent-up anger from the preceding three years of record company sabotage and missed opportunities came spewing out in one five minute torrent of adrenalin and breathless abandon.

Best. Opening. Song. *Ever*.

'Stay Clean' (Clarke/Kilmister/Taylor)
When you have started with a masterpiece of speed and precision, it's almost impossible to follow it up. Mind you, Philthy sets his mark high and opens this tune with another hefty battering of his kit before allowing the cheeky riff to enter the fray and then settling into a pounding groove that has a nicely melodic turn to it. Lyrically, Lemmy has already started railing against people who lie and cheat and exhorts the listener to stick to their principles and their truth as no one can rely on other people to back you up (it's no stretch to suggest he is talking about record company executives here). The best way to avoid chipping away at your soul is to stay true to yourself, thus remaining 'clean'.

Thankfully, it isn't about your Mum or Dad bending your ear to go and have a bath.

'(I Won't) Pay Your Price' (Clarke/Kilmister/Taylor)
A rather choppy riff greets the listener and barely lets up until the end. Eddie seems determined to throw in a solo at every opportunity (one wonders how Lemmy found any room to actually sing) while Lemmy shouts about kicking someone out of a relationship and listing all the reasons why they need to go. It's blunt and it doesn't pull any punches, but it is honest and world-weary and just a little hot-headed, which feels remarkably accurate in the situation it is describing.

'I'll Be Your Sister' (Clarke/Kilmister/Taylor)
Well, the comedy had to stake its claim soon enough. The words are basically a desperate man's chat-up lines set to music. The character in the song will be anything to get laid, including being someone's mother or, as the title suggests, sister. Sometimes these are not deeply philosophical lyrics.

An energetic bass rumble starts proceedings and then the band chuck in a dirty riff and another drum pounding (although Philthy gets to thrash his cymbals too) before the lyrics are bellowed out in a somewhat disappointing manner. Jimmy Miller obviously has a great handle on the musical side of things but is beginning to highlight that producing a great vocal performance is not his forte.

'Capricorn' (Clarke/Kilmister/Taylor)

Although Lemmy eschewed all fakery and quack medicines, preferring science to superstition, he did have a blind spot when it came to astrology, and this is the proof. Here he writes a lyric about his own astrological sign and the disappointment of being born on Christmas Eve. He almost writes his own epitaph in the first few lines:

> A thousand nights, I've spent alone
> Solitaire, to the bone
> But I don't mind, I'm my own best friend
> From the beginning, to the end

Musically this slows the pace to a trot, although it exhibits the same musical moves as previous songs and has some beautiful guitar notes and lines which really add to the atmosphere, butting up to the chorus as if they had been composed with these words in mind. Eddie excels at this melancholic blues material, showcasing his rather more emotive and soulful side. Philthy, curiously, appears to be playing 'Overkill' at half speed, but it suits the mood, the genuine attempt at singing from Lemmy and the echoing guitar that graces the fade out. It turns out, this is surprisingly touching from a band with Motörhead's image.

'No Class' (Clarke/Kilmister/Taylor)

Venting his anger at the people who had mocked and belittled himself and his band, Lemmy pours out a vitriolic lyric sarcastically repeating all the insults that had been levelled at them. He turns it around in the final verse by suggesting the nay-sayers are the ones with no class. A staunchly punk-infused rant that batters the listener with its throat-scratching vocals, the defining characteristic is the crunchy riff supplied by Eddie and the single cock-eyed guitar solo that he drops in as a sop to the rock crowd. Eddie plays it straight here and doesn't let go of the basic rock and roll riff that powers this thumping juggernaut. Ironically, when this was covered a few years later by Wendy O Williams, she brought a shrieking screech to the vocals that almost entirely outdo Lemmy but rather highlight the line: 'too much, too soon, you know you're really out of tune'. Something that Eddie was happy to agree with at the time. While not the most musically accomplished of songs, the sheer nerve of the tune finds little to better it in the competitors around at the time.

'Damage Case' (Clarke/Farren/Kilmister/Taylor)

Embracing the ferocious bass work and slightly off-kilter guitar, this short but barbaric crash and thud of a song portrays a mangled mind in search of a human connection. They find themselves ostracised because of their condition and, in the end, cannot find the companionship and love they need. Admittedly, knowing Lemmy, this might equally be a semi-autobiographical take on not being able to get off with a woman due to his looks and demeanour. It's a cracking little brute of a song all the same.

Mick Farren gets a last and unexpected writing credit here for penning at least some (if not all) of the lyrics.

'Tear Ya Down' (Clarke/Kilmister/Taylor)

This remixed version of the 'Louie Louie' b-side, produced by the little-known Neil Richmond, was added to the album as it was running short. Barely clocking in at just over half an hour, the band were happy for its inclusion as they thought it could do with a little more exposure. It was remixed by Jimmy Miller to help it blend in sonically with the rest of the tracks here. Lemmy, of course, is singing about his favourite subject: chatting up women and taking them to bed. There's not much to the lyric, but he invests it with the required licentious vocal and the band surge through the vibrating riff and quick-fire solos with ease. Starting with a shouted 'eins, zwei, drei, vier' from Lemmy, this is the first real evidence of his lifelong interest in Germany and its history (even at this stage, he was already somewhat infamous for wearing an Iron Cross).

'Metropolis' (Clarke/Kilmister/Taylor)

Appropriating the title from the German 1927 silent science fiction movie, this is a trundling lope that references the film but also articulates Lemmy's reactions to London when he first moved there. Eddie gets to throw more of his sharp solos into the mix and the band showcases their restraint on this corking mid-tempo delight.

Many years later, the group released a live version for a one-off freebie single for their Greek fans, which they inevitably renamed 'Acropolis'! A consistent live highlight, the song allows the entire band a breather before they redouble their efforts and race for the end of the set.

'Limb From Limb' (Clarke/Kilmister/Taylor)

Taking note of the poor closing track on their debut, this is the start of the crashing finales set to grace a host of future collections. There is a blues gait to the throbbing music and an air of broken machismo in the lyrics, which could leave you worrying about the state of Lemmy's self-esteem but, just when the song seems about to fade out, the band pull the rug out from underneath the listener and speed up for the big finish. That 'we're-playing-this-live-in-the-studio' ending was done to death on their debut, but they still insist on pulling that cliché out, and not for the last time.

Related recordings
'Too Late Too Late' (Clarke/Kilmister/Taylor)

Ostensibly about a cheating partner and the need for the protagonist to eject the person from their life, this has quite a subtext when it is seen in the light of all the record company shenanigans the band had to deal with before this album. Lemmy found this vitriolic broadside confined to a b-side, although it would have fitted the album brilliantly. Eddie lays down a staggering riff that becomes an earworm almost immediately, and then he adds an echoed solo that raises the song a notch. Lemmy puts his larynx into overdrive for the chorus and then finds his voice echoing as well, giving it just that little psychedelic twist as the song fades away.

'Like A Nightmare' (Clarke/Kilmister/Taylor)

Relegated to another b-side, this has a gargled vocal (complete with tin can echo) and a garbled lyric, but the music is undeniably strong with a strident riff from Eddie, a chugging bassline and some neat drumming from the always expressive Philthy. Eddie seems to go for one solo too many, but this had a place just waiting for it on the main release. Why it didn't replace 'Tear Ya Down' is anybody's guess.

Bomber (Bronze, October 1979)

Personnel:
Lemmy Kilmister: vocals, bass
Fast Eddie Clarke: guitars
Philthy Animal Taylor: drums
Produced at Roundhouse and Olympic Studios, London, July-August 1979 by
Jimmy Miller.
Highest chart place: UK: 12
Running time (approximate): 36:48

Touring the album ensured that both it, and the title track single actually entered the Top 40 and the band were ecstatic. The reception from the wider record-buying public, as well as the live audiences, was gratifying and it seemed Motörhead had finally turned a corner in their fortunes, so the record company asked for another album as quickly as possible. Already used to working to tight deadlines, the band were not to know that they would be releasing two albums in one year.

By all accounts, the rehearsal and writing sessions were straightforward and lacked any more dramas, although Lemmy was disappointed that the songs couldn't be road-tested as they had been for the debut.

However, he had plans for something spectacular for their stage set, based on one of the newly written songs, and he was in a positive mood when they commenced the sessions. Bronze had decided that Jimmy Miller was a safe pair of hands and contracted him as producer for a second time. The album was delivered so quickly that the record company released it early to capitalise on the band's increased profile.

'Dead Men Tell No Tales' (Clarke/Kilmister/Taylor)

Lemmy was already a vocal critic of heroin when he penned the words to this vitriolic attack on the drug. According to his autobiography, heroin had killed Sue, the first love of his life, and he remained virulently opposed to the drug until the day he died.

During the recording of this album, it became quite apparent that Jimmy was back using heroin (having been introduced to it while working with the Rolling Stones), turning up extremely late to sessions and providing little input to the songs as they had been constructed. Bearing in mind the modus operandi of the band when recording, Lemmy was able to write a stinging rebuke to Jimmy and sing it to his face from the studio. The session must have been surreal to observe: Jimmy wandering about the control room in a daze, Lemmy viciously singing his disgust through the window. Lemmy was never one to hold back on his opinions. In November 2003, he was invited to speak to the Welsh Assembly about the dangers of heroin. The Conservative AM (Assembly Member) who had extended the invite got a surprisingly mundane speech from Lemmy but found himself entirely nonplussed with the following question and answer session where Lemmy provided his own answer to the problem:

> I hate the idea, even as I say it, but I do believe the only way to treat heroin is to legalise it.

He wanted to ensure it was safe for people to use, rather than mixed with bleach or rat poison. The AM gave a rictus grin at this point, silently acknowledging that Lemmy had gone entirely off-script with this remark. Astonishingly, Lemmy was never asked back for a return visit.

'Dead Men Tell No Tales' is undoubtedly from Lemmy's viewpoint and the blazing vituperation of the words is, thankfully, matched by the serious crunch of the music and the top end soloing from Eddie. By the third verse, Lemmy spells it out for Jimmy:

> You used to be my friend,
> But that friendship's coming to an end,
> My meaning must be clear,
> You know pity is all that you hear,
> But if you are doing smack,
> You won't be coming back...

There are some strange shouts and yowls that pepper the song, but the intent couldn't be more explicit. The band would not work with Jimmy again, although they were happy to acknowledge his influence on *Overkill*.

'Lawman' (Clarke/Kilmister/Taylor)

Strapped to a mid-tempo head-nodding beat, Lemmy expounds his thoughts on the police and law and order. His chorus vocal emulates, and rides roughshod over, the sparkling guitar lick that Eddie lays down, and it is the sign of a tight-knit group that Eddie's ego wasn't troubled by this cover-up. 'Lawman' is a sturdy album cut but doesn't have the in-your-face quality that characterises a great Motörhead song.

The first hints of the 'cowboy desperadoes' persona that was to follow begins on this album. Many of the titles are inspired by Lemmy's fondness for the American outlaw image, even if the lyrics tell a different story. Eddie adds a nice facsimile of a slide guitar to the later stages, giving it that Americana flavour.

The fade-out mixes into the next track...

'Sweet Revenge' (Clarke/Kilmister/Taylor)

Although a simple production trick, this modest tale of murderous retribution starts with drawkcab drums and a worrying greeting of 'Hello victims!' before loping into a walking pace plod that has a disciplined descending guitar flourish to recommend it. To add to the fun, Eddie performs a drawkcab guitar solo which gives the song the sinister edge that it so evidently requires.

There's more than a hint that this disturbing lyric could also be read as a commentary on the aftermath of Lemmy's firing from Hawkwind four years earlier. Change murder and mutilation to sleeping with the band's wives and girlfriends and the meaning becomes obvious. It doesn't help that he sings the words with such relish, even if the recording of his vocal isn't multi-tracked and sounds like he has his head in a biscuit barrel.

'Sharpshooter' (Clarke/Kilmister/Taylor)
Rather more concerned with contract assassins and mercenaries than cowboy sharpshooters, this track, nevertheless, pounds along in chugging fashion, although it spends precious little time establishing itself before fading out. Almost as if the band themselves believed it was so perfunctory that they said 'right, on to the next one'...

'Poison' (Clarke/Kilmister/Taylor)
Lemmy seems to have found a strong well of inspiration for the majority of the words on this album. Lemmy did not have a comfortable childhood, but that provides great material for lyrics. A heartfelt diatribe about marriage, Lemmy harnesses the burning injustice of his father, leaving him at an early age and abandoning his wife at the same time.
The third verse, again, makes his feelings plain:

> My Father; he used to be a preacher,
> Never taught me nothing but scorn,
> If I ever catch him on the street, yeah,
> I'm gonna make him wish he'd never been born,
> He was poison,
> Guess he poisoned my life,
> He was poison,
> I wish my mother wasn't his wife, no!

Lemmy never forgave him. Interestingly, when Lemmy found out that he had a son from a brief liaison, many years later, he actively sought the boy out and tried to behave like the father he never had. Lemmy had been scarred by his experience and was determined not to make the same mistake. His son, Paul Inder, appears in the documentary film *Lemmy* and is genuinely startled when Lemmy describes him as the most precious thing in his apartment.

Musically upping the pace and barrelling in with a neat little riff, the body of the song soon changes direction with a second, not so memorable, riff replacing the first. Eddie drags the first riff back for the faded finale, but it's a shame they couldn't work out how to keep that initial riff as the centre of attention. The bass is prominent and bounces along in a style that recalls no one as much as Steve Harris of Iron Maiden (they were at the very beginning of their career and had yet to record their debut album when *Bomber* was released). The chorus has an echoed vocal of 'poison', which seems to come from Eddie and it is awful. It sounds like he is shouting in the corridor as if he meant to bellow 'fire' instead.

'Stone Dead Forever' (Clarke/Kilmister/Taylor)
One of the greatest Motörhead songs ever written; this hand grenade of a tune blasts the cobwebs of the slow-paced rockers preceding it into fragments. The lyrics lambast politicians, greedheads and record company executives in equal measure and proved so inspiring that Lemmy felt compelled to reuse parts of it for 'Just 'Cos You Got The Power' eight years later.

The growling bass sound returns, but the first few moments tend to drag while the rest of the band seem to be finding their feet. Once that is over, Eddie barges in with a quite breathtaking riff and everyone seems to catch up and get on board. From here on, there are no mistakes, only bruising rock and roll played as if lives depended on it. Playing with the same humorous thoughts, the title was given a small tweak and then reclaimed for the 2003 box set *Stone Deaf Forever*, which is an equally silly title (but undoubtedly true!).

Making a habit of putting the best verse third, Lemmy sings:

You're a financial wizard, yeah, you're a top tycoon
You're a sweet lounge lizard with a silver spoon
You know you've never had it quite so good
And you didn't know that you even could
But your time has come today
Turns out your feet are clay
Whatever happened to your life
Stone dead forever

The band tear through this with joy and exuberance, highlighting the sometimes disappointing musical backing to some of the other songs here. Eddie throws in a storming solo and then carries on firing off little bundles of guitar notes just because he can.

'All The Aces' (Clarke/Kilmister/Taylor)
Figuring that once is never enough, Lemmy takes another withering look at managers, record executives and the wider world. Essentially about the venal, shallow nature of showbusiness and the servitude that most musicians were contracted under, Lemmy rails against the iniquities and inequities of his position. The businessmen (and, with the best will in the world, they were all men at this time) have the protagonist's career, almost their life, in their hands. Lemmy refers to them as 'sly', 'parasites', 'people who ain't got no faces' and they 'make me vomit' while he spends his time asking just where the money

has gone. It's a very old story in the music industry (Lemmy's rock and roll heroes suffered particularly harshly early on), although matters have improved with the passing of time.

A classy riff gets rather over-repeated, unfortunately, but it stands up reasonably well to its companions here, which are all essentially looking for the producer to pull these songs together into something better. For the most part, the songs on *Bomber* sound like discarded album cuts from *Overkill*, although the lyrics have improved tremendously, mostly because Lemmy was angry and that often proved inspirational.

'Step Down' (Clarke/Kilmister/Taylor)

There's a moment at the beginning of this song where it seems like a different band have accidentally been recorded. After a long introductory lope, this flabby blues-rock track seems to revel in cliché without once breaking out of its disappointing resemblance to several hundred other songs. There are distinct hints of the future Fastway albums here. Featuring a perfectly phrased but some what undistinguished vocal from Eddie, where he sounds like he's channelling a sub-par AOR version of Glenn Hughes, it also boasts a lyric that would normally be discarded from the back of an envelope, never mind make it to recorded status. There's a reasonable assumption that these were actually written by Eddie and it shows. Lemmy later noted that Eddie had been griping about his lack of exposure within the band and wanted to be at the front of the stage now and then. Lemmy took Eddie literally and forced him to sing on the album and it was played live a few times before Eddie departed. Unfortunately, it sounds like a song from a bygone era when blues-rock ruled the world, illustrating how far music had progressed in the meantime. Eddie thinks it is 1972, Lemmy knows it is 1979 and Philthy knows ...very little except how to have a good time.

'Talking Head' (Clarke/Kilmister/Taylor)

A reverse double entendre, a rarity in the Motörhead canon, this is a sarcastic attack on television news, propaganda and the influence that politicians have on the media. It can't be a coincidence that the words are just as relevant today as they ever were. Driven by Lemmy's speaker-weakening bass and a sudden desire to charge for the finishing line, there are signs that the band were even more pushed for time than usual. Lemmy misses the odd word in the lyrics and slurs in a couple of places to disguise the fact that the words don't entirely fit, while Eddie sounds like he did the solos in a single take. Only Philthy sounds in control all the time, but he would have recorded his parts earlier in the sessions.

On the plus side, there is a crackling riff that still sounds fresh as a newborn and the trio are clearly enjoying themselves.

'Bomber' (Clarke/Kilmister/Taylor)

Obviously, this was written as a tail-end tune to send everyone scurrying home with the sound of battle in their ears, Motörhead closing on a corker of a song. Lemmy had read Len Deighton's seminal 1970 novel concerning the fictional 'last flight of an RAF bomber over Germany on the night of June 31st 1943' (the date being deliberately nonsensical to ensure no one could accuse Len of plagiarism) and was a huge fan. Lemmy was well known for reading voraciously about war, in both fact and fiction, and found himself inspired by this remarkable tome.

Eddie chucks a 1000mph rock and roll riff out and Philthy surges forward in reply, throwing all his energy into the drumming, while Lemmy croak-shouts every last syllable and hammers at his bass in order to keep up with the double kick drums pounding ahead.'Bomber' lacks any finesse or sweetness, but it captures the adrenaline-soaked glory of Motörhead in their prime.

Not only that, but Lemmy had other plans up his denim sleeve: he envisaged an extraordinary lighting rig in the shape of a skeletal bomber, which could be raised and lowered to imitate an aircraft in flight. It was designed and built and, when in use, it looked fantastic, impressively dominating the stage set. Lemmy had his wish and audiences around the world had a searing memory to take away with them. It is impossible to miss as it has a commanding presence on the cover photo to *No Sleep 'til Hammersmith*, just as it overshadowed the stage.

By a not very startling 'coincidence,' this song is also a sneaky reference to 'black bombers', which were the street name for the amphetamines that Lemmy took from the 1960s to the mid-1980s. Following the ceasing of their manufacture, speed-freaks had to find alternative sources of supply for their drug of choice, although these turned out to be relatively easily replaced, luckily for Lemmy.

Related recordings
'Over The Top' (Clarke/Kilmister/Taylor)
Early in Motörhead's career, songs were sometimes written at soundchecks and in rehearsals before they were committed to tape. This is one such track, which ended up as a neglected b-side. This version was recorded by the full trio during the sessions for the album. Lemmy, however, had found himself deputising in The Damned during 1979 and ended up in a studio with them in May. They recorded a cover of Sweet's 'Ballroom Blitz' with Lemmy on bass duties. Looking for a b-side for a projected MotorDamn single (Lemmy was apparently already thinking about collaborations, even at this early stage) he offered this new tune-up for consideration. The Damned said 'yes' and the first version was duly recorded. Unfortunately, The Damned had even more trouble with record companies than Motörhead did and the single was never released. The MotorDamn (or the name could have been MotorDam, no one seems entirely sure now) version snuck out later on, fulfilling bonus track duties on reissues by both The Damned and Lemmy.

Motörhead offer up a sterling re-recording this time which would have suited the album far more than a couple of the songs that made it ('Step Down' anyone?) even though it starts in a fairly ramshackle manner. It has all the thrust and panache that a lot of the album lacks, although it still finishes with the corny live thrash-about beloved of rock bands everywhere. Lyrically this is off-the-cuff stuff which basically says the band are 'mad' and, er, 'over the top'. It contains, amongst other nonsense, the immortal lines:

You know it's no lie, my main alibi
It's a waste of time
You know it's the truth, the lyrics the proof
And at least it rhymes

You can have me, 'cos I'm barmy
Completely
Over the top, over the top, over the top

The listening world may have thought they had abandoned this orphan song, but they went so far as to re-present it live in 2012, though it obviously had very little to say in relation to the Olympic Games taking place that year.

Ace Of Spades (Bronze, November 1980)

Personnel:
Lemmy Kilmister: vocals, bass
Fast Eddie Clarke: guitars
Philthy Animal Taylor: drums
Produced at Jackson's Studios, Rickmansworth, August-September 1980 by Vic Maile.
Highest chart place: UK: 4
Running time (approximate): 36:42

There are some unexpected references to the band in the wider world, even at this early stage. In 1980 *The Blues Brothers* musical was a huge cult film and it featured the use of the word Motörhead in its original context, meaning speed freak. A couple of scenes later, a 'Lemmy's' fast food restaurant is prominently placed in the background. This cannot be a coincidence! The film itself contains a great deal of the music Lemmy loved (rock and roll, blues, r & b and more), although it surprisingly predates *Ace of Spades*.

At this point, United Artists realised their mistake and hurriedly put out *On Parole*, figuring that they would ride the wave of Motörhead fever. As it was, the album charted at #65 and didn't stay around for long, although it probably enabled Larry Wallis to gain some useful royalties from it. The current line-up didn't have any say in the issuing of the album and disowned the record entirely, only commenting that they were long past that phase of their career.

While Bronze were watching Motörhead exhaustively touring, and waiting for the next album (impatient buggers), they followed up the 'Bomber' single with the worryingly titled *Golden Years EP*, a set of four live songs put out as a makeshift measure to keeps the band's name in the public eye. It was a surprise hit, even with 'Leavin' Here' placed as the lead track, and reached the Top 10. It showed the live prowess of the band and the ease with which they could translate the studio tracks to the stage, but it was hardly essential.

When work eventually commenced on the new album, the first port of call was a sandstone quarry in Barnet, London (and not an American or African desert, as people believed) for the cover shoot. They duly adopted their Cowboy personas and pretended to be outlaws for the day. The sky was overcast on the day the pictures were taken, so a further piece of trickery was employed and the grey clouds were replaced with fluffy white clouds and blue sky.

Lemmy had been a fan of Vic Maile since he had recorded and mixed Hawkwind's landmark *Space Ritual* double live album in 1973 (on which Lemmy cemented his bass playing reputation) and, finally, he was able to persuade Bronze that Vic was the man for the job of producing their next, eagerly anticipated, album.

38

'Ace Of Spades' (Clarke/Kilmister/Taylor)

Although accepted now as the definitive Motörhead anthem, this scuzzy slice of rock and roll was initially an also-ran in the band's mind. It's rare that a band would place their most significant track at the head of an album and that's because the group were happy with the outcome but didn't think it had staying power, suggesting that it sounded a little too commercial. Everybody is wrong sometimes, but this takes the biscuit, throws it to the floor and crushes it underfoot until it disappears into the cracks of the flagstones. Lemmy thought he was saddled with the song for life but, as he says in the sleeve notes on the live release *Everything Louder Than Everyone Else*:

I got to hate this number, but then I got to like it again, so here it is!

'Ace of Spades' is quintessential Motörhead. From the overdriven opening bass through the ultra punk-infused body of the song to the glorious ending, it just oozes, well, sweat and booze and speed, to be honest. Even the middle eight sounds ferocious and that is after Lemmy famously dubbed it 'the tap-dancing section'!

The ultimate gambling song (the line 'the pleasure is to play' has been adopted by at least one online gambling company) there is a reference to the notorious poker game where Wild Bill Hickok was shot and killed while he held 'the dead man's hand' of aces and eights. Lemmy would go on to get a lot of mileage from this subject matter, although he always exhibited his gambling method of choice as the ubiquitous fruit machines of which he was so fond. The interlocking of the words with the music reaches a highpoint here and, if you listen carefully, you can hear Lemmy singing and enunciating each word instead of shouting the lyrics. Probably, this was why the music disappears behind Lemmy's sandpaper vocals for a line before returning for a loose guitar solo and a rare proper ending for a tune. Much of this was down to Vic's influence as he reminded Lemmy during the sessions that he could actually sing and pushed the band to both tighten up and stretch out during the writing phase. In addition, after the quick takes of the first three albums (the band thinking that any more than four takes took the spontaneity out of a song), Vic also insisted that the band played the tune until it was the best it could be rather than settling for something that sounded 'good enough'.

Becoming an unlikely hit single, the ensuing multi-media presence of the band (that's television, radio and newspapers for the younger audience out there; in 1980, the internet and social media was science fiction land) ensured their profile soared into the stratosphere.

As well as playing it every night, first in the main setlist and then as a perpetual encore, the band were not averse to hiring the song out to all and sundry. It has graced several TV adverts, been used as a featured song on many TV programmes (e.g. *The Young Ones* in 1984 and *Black Books* in 2004) and provided many films and shows with scorching background music. When the advertising company responsible for Kronenbourg 1664 lager approached the band in 2010, it was with a different idea in mind: to recreate the song in an acoustic setting. Given the money on offer, and the chance to radically reinterpret a song that sometimes felt like an albatross, Motörhead jumped at the chance. The result is surprisingly in keeping with the original and really benefits from the reinvention.

'Love Me Like A Reptile' (Clarke/Kilmister/Taylor)
Boasting a hummable tune and a cracking chorus, this had Lemmy laughing at his own silliness. The lyrics were made up in a few minutes (by some accounts while he was in the toilet at the studio) but sent him off chuckling, so he knew he had to record it. Taking the piss out of macho posturing, Lemmy coined probably the first song ostensibly about lying down with a cold-blooded partner. It's no wonder Lemmy quietly thought of Motörhead as a comedy group on occasion. Not every lyric is momentously earnest and so, chucking in a line like: 'scaly baby, see you shine', is a bit of a giveaway that Lemmy had been chortling wildly to himself.

The knockabout joy of the tune is matched by the bonkers words that are attached to it, this is Motörhead saying don't take life so seriously. The amped-up rock and roll riff that permeates the whole song says much the same thing.

'Shoot You In The Back' (Clarke/Kilmister/Taylor)
Philthy's influence must have wormed its way into Lemmy's subconscious (Philthy was the one with the fetish for the band dressing as cowboys for the cover shoot) because this is another self-mythologising cowboy influenced lyric which starts with:

Western movies!
The riders ride, into the night
Into the west, to see whose gun's the best

And leads on to a tale of outlaws and ambush where the bad guy definitely wears black.

It's coupled to a tiger claw riff so remarkable it seems that Eddie has tapped a new well of inspiration. It gallops along with only Philthy's drum splatter (overused even on the debut version of 'Motörhead') and the 'live' crash and wallop ending making it feel over-played. Ironically, Philthy praised Vic for toning down his drum rolls and excesses, taking on board Vic's desire to simplify the arrangements so that the songs could win through.

'Live To Win' (Clarke/Kilmister/Taylor)
Lemmy gets both philosophical and political here, urging everyone to understand that simply being alive is winning. He had it tattooed on himself ('Born To Lose, Live To Win'), he had it written on his bass and he absolutely believed it. The last few lines encapsulate his thinking:

Break down the wall,
Live it up, it's their time to fall,
Anarchy is coming in,
If you know we Live To Win.

The opening bass riff has echoes of other tunes, but the rock and roll charge that pounces out of the speakers is all Motörhead. Unfortunately, Eddie spends much of his time towards the latter stages of the tune soloing endlessly and the brevity that the song deserved is rather fattened up. Short, as many punk bands will tell you, is good.

'Fast and Loose' (Clarke/Kilmister/Taylor)
Describing both the band and their preferred female company, the tricksy but catchy riff is harnessed to a cantering pace that only lets up after the solo (introduced by Lemmy with the words 'no remorse!' for some reason) and it ends with Lemmy's multi-tracked harmony vocals simulating a duet with himself that is both hummable and strangely impressive. Eddie keeps his soloing brief and snappy and the entire tune is over much too soon, probably because they are approaching the last song of side one and need the room.

'(We Are) The Road Crew' (Clarke/Kilmister/Taylor)
In an inspired moment, Lemmy paid tribute to the normally invisible and unsung members of any touring band's entourage: the road crew. From the lighting rigs to the sound engineers to the people who ensure the instruments are in the correct place and in working order through to the caterers, tour managers, stagehands and all the way down to the humpers and shovers, Lemmy penned a few words that have been known to make grown roadies cry.

Philthy remarked that he thought the music to this song was extremely difficult to write words to. Lemmy replied with some of the most autobiographical lyrics ever to grace a tune. He also endeared himself to every road crew in the world and, having been a roadie, he knew exactly how tough and demanding and exhausting the role was. To make it even more memorable, he put one of his strongest choruses in and married it to the throbbing roll of the music, which sounded like heavy trucks barrelling through the night.

Eddie throws in a squalling and feedback-laden solo for the end run and then it all fades out, another masterpiece captured on tape.

'Fire, Fire' (Clarke/Kilmister/Taylor)
Ignored, even at the time, this is mid-range Motörhead on autopilot. The words are either a sly and sarcastic commentary on macho posturing or a pitifully lame attempt to boost the egos of the band members. The words don't quite fit the music, the chorus is especially scrappy (is that Eddie throwing in his kitchen shout at the back?), and the incendiary use of the word 'holocaust'

seems both needlessly provocative and pointlessly dramatic. Perhaps the incipient success on the horizon of their career encouraged Lemmy to be a little too forthright and much too insensitive.

It has a marvellously forceful and bludgeoning main riff, though. Musically this has little to fault it and its absence from succeeding live tours is notable.

'Jailbait' (Clarke/Kilmister/Taylor)

Even the title is an unsubtle paean to young groupies and, within the current climate of child exploitation and abuse, this is one lyric that has not stood the test of time. There wasn't a lot to recommend it even then (it has a lewd *Lolita* undercurrent to it, which is disturbingly summed up in the lines:

I don't even dare to ask your age,
It's enough to know you're here backstage

... and the rest of the lyrics fare little better). This is undoubtedly based on real-life, and groupies remain a common sight, but the argument that they are there of their own free will doesn't excuse any of the thoughts expressed here. Years later, Lemmy would distance himself from these sentiments and wrote 'Don't Let Daddy Kiss Me' as his personal response to changing attitudes.

Musically, of course, this is another barnstorming trip through Motörhead's remarkable riff-generating engine and it powers along in galumphing style. It is an undoubted success from Eddie's viewpoint and it has a truly captivating riff that would be greeted with delight by any rock band that came up with it. Most second-rate rock bands strive and fail to produce such a riff in their entire careers.

The words, however, are a bitter taste on top of a sweet confection. The world has, thankfully, moved on.

'Dance' (Clarke/Kilmister/Taylor)

Eddie always said that he disliked this tune because he felt it was too poppy and commercial, and that was before the lyrics were added! It's a simple tribute to the rock and roll dancing of Lemmy's youth and it sounds like it. Apart from Eddie's finger-blistering solos, this is a basic stomp through the nightclubs of the late 1950s, just as it emerges into the more widescreen 1960s.

Commerciality aside, the chorus uses the same structure as 'Fire Fire', only this time it is Lemmy hollering in the distance. Philthy was once asked to sing backing vocals for a Motörhead song, but Lemmy was heard to proclaim that Philthy sang like 'two cats being stapled together,' and that was the end of his singing career! On the 'Dance' and 'Fire Fire' backup choruses, it wouldn't have made much difference if Philthy *had* sung.

'Bite The Bullet' (Clarke/Kilmister/Taylor)

A simple breaking-up song (although it takes the protagonist three verses to screw up his courage and actually leave) attached to a punishing and decidedly metal riff, this is the shortest tune here and it leads, without pause, into the next song. As an album morsel, it is great; as a full song, it lacks a killer chorus and individuality.

'The Chase Is Better Than The Catch' (Clarke/Kilmister/Taylor)

The band knew this song as 'the face is better than the snatch', which wouldn't win them any awards for enlightened thinking (but at least it's not about underage girls). Lemmy acknowledged the lecherously Neanderthal nature of his lyrics in the sleeve notes to *Everything Louder Than Everyone Else*: 'this is the sexist one!!' but it is, at least, a little more tongue in cheek (feel free to add your own double entendre here!) than some of the surrounding lyrics.

A fuzzy chiming guitar riff disguises the shuffle underbeat that carries this mid-tempo tune into the realms of greatness. While the words are highly unlikely to win awards, the tune is another triumph, even though it has several shared musical elements with 'Shoot You In The Back', including at least one of the riffs.

'The Hammer' (Clarke/Kilmister/Taylor)

This is just a crushing example of why the band was sometimes grouped in with the New Wave Of British Heavy Metal that counted Iron Maiden and Saxon amongst their number. Lemmy declined to be pigeon-holed so easily and always asserted that he felt more akin to punk and, indeed, rock and roll than any of the heavy metal groups. Mind you, that didn't stop him from offering up cover versions of some of these artists when he was asked.

This closes the album in bruising style and illustrates a more pessimistic outlook from Lemmy's pen, suggesting that the titular hammer will bludgeon everything into dust, regardless of what people do with their lives. Its nihilistic stance counts as a partial summation of the album's lyrics, while the music pounds the hammer in aural agreement. The punishment of the instruments and the combined force of their playing ends proceedings on a battering note that suggests a heavier direction is in the offing.

Related recordings

'Dirty Love' (Clarke/Kilmister/Taylor)

Beautifully loose in execution and wholly deserving of a place on the album, this neglected b-side is prime Motörhead and doesn't hesitate to hit 'echo' on the chorus vocals or take advantage of a neat spiralling riff from Eddie. There is even a hint of psychedelia in Eddie's guitar gyrations and *Ace of Spades* might have ended up a very different album if this had been exchanged for one of the less successful songs that adorned side two. The lyrics are back to their ridiculous best and both instrumentally and vocally, the band exhibit a joie de vivre that is in marked contrast to a couple of the more sober or disappointing songs slapped onto the album.

St Valentine's Day Massacre EP

Personnel:
Lemmy Kilmister: vocals, bass
Fast Eddie Clarke: guitars
Kelly Johnson: guitars, vocals
Kim McAuliffe: rhythm guitar
Enid Williams: bass
Denise Dufort: drums
Produced at Jackson's Studios, London, December 1980 by Vic Maile.
Highest chart place: UK: 5
Running time (approximate): 9:36

The band set out on the road with label mates Girlschool to promote *Ace of Spades* far and wide. However, upon its release on an unsuspecting world, Philthy had to go and break his neck. He was dropped on his head by a friend during a test of strength. With all the live shows and other commitments that were in place, Philthy had to press on, which is why he is sporting a neck brace in the 'Ace Of Spades' video and wore it on the following tour. A lump eventually became visible on the back of his neck (calcium deposits arising from the spinal trauma) and the protrusion was affectionately nicknamed his 'knob'.Denise Dufort of Girlschool was approached to see if she could double up with the headliners as drummer, but this proved impractical. Nevertheless, desiring to work together, a thought came into someone's head...

'Please Don't Touch' (Frederick Heath [Johnny Kidd]/Guy Robinson)

Blazing a trail through their touring obligations, the bands joined together in the studio when they had a short window in the schedule, reuniting with Vic Maile for the occasion. Lemmy was a huge fan of Johnny Kidd & the Pirates and he recommended their 1959 debut single as the ideal opportunity for Motörhead and Girlschool to, ahem, come together. Lemmy was extolling the virtues of Kelly Johnson's guitar playing to anyone who would listen (to such an extent that Eddie may well have thought his job was at risk) and was quite taken with Denise Dufort's heavy-hitting drum technique. Denise, in fact, drums on all the songs on the EP (regardless of whether it is credited to Motörhead, HeadGirl or Girlschool) as Philthy was unavailable for the recording. Philthy was always one step away from A&E...

Staying true to their aim of playing rock and roll at 1000mph, this somewhat unfaithful cover sprints along impressively without betraying its musical roots for one second. The sheer speed at which this is taken, however, puts this version firmly in the present rather than producing a dusty relic from the past. It has that early Elvis Presley stutter beat, the patented sound of 1950s guitars and the vocal mannerisms of the era spot on. Both Kelly and Eddie take a solo each and the whole enterprise sounds like enormous fun was had by all,

Lemmy's throaty growl mingling salaciously with Kim McAuliffe's inevitably sweeter tones. Although uncredited, there seems to be a piano at work here too. This was a massively unexpected chart hit (it went Top Five) and, coincidentally, bolstered Lemmy's belief that rock and roll would live forever.

'Emergency' (Denise Dufort/Kelly Johnson/Kim McAuliffe/Enid Williams)

Thinking that they would need a b-side or two for the single, the idea was mooted that each band should do a cover of the other. Girlschool chose 'Bomber' and gave it a decent workout, Motörhead chose 'Emergency' and, ironically, Philthy missed out on contributing to this rousing cover of the Girlschool standout because he was in accident and emergency at the time!

Offering up a memorable chorus and some nifty songwriting, strangely, it is Eddie who provides the verse vocals while Lemmy only joins in on the chorus. Denise is a more than capable substitute for Philthy and provides some epic sounding drumming. The song starts and ends with an air raid siren rather than the emergency services alarm bells, which gives it a greater sense of tension and drama.

Lemmy, and other members of the band, would go on to work with Girlschool on many further occasions. Lemmy was the epitome of a dichotomy where, although he was undoubtedly sexist lyrically, he remained a largely unsung supporter of women's rights both within music and without. It was a paradox that Lemmy never entirely managed to bridge.

Iron Fist (Bronze, April 1982)

Personnel:
Lemmy Kilmister: vocals, bass
Fast Eddie Clarke: guitars
Philthy Animal Taylor: drums
Produced at Ramport and Morgan Studios, London, January-February 1982 by Will
Reid Dick and Fast Eddie Clarke.
Highest chart place: UK: 6
Running time (approximate): 36:24

By 1981 Motörhead were already a household name in any household that
was worthy of the name. This was just the right time to unleash their first live
album on the world and the incomparable *No Sleep 'til Hammersmith* was the
result. A chart-topping lion's roar that comprehensively revitalised the older
songs featured into their definitive forms and provided a fantastic glimpse of
the road carnage and blistering live juggernaut the band had become. Arguably,
this is the only live album of theirs that a listener *needs* to own.

Unfortunately, as Lemmy noted in retrospect, the only way forward after this
extraordinary success was down. The decision to allow Eddie and his engineer
chum Will Reid Dick (renowned for his work on several hugely successful Thin
Lizzy albums) to produce the album was only the first in a series of mistakes
that would quickly lead to Eddie's estrangement and then resignation and a
further reduction in the band's fortunes.

'Iron Fist' (Clarke/Kilmister/Taylor)

This opener sets out the stall for the next twelve sloppy and under-rehearsed
songs that follow. Glimmers of Lemmy's lyrical ability are visible throughout,
but the whole collection suffers from the under-achievement of arrogance,
following a top-four studio album and a number one live album, and
Motörhead are clearly coasting here. Placed as the lead-off single, this actually
gave listeners a fine first impression of the album, despite the harsh and tinny
production job and the lyrics-by-numbers feeling. If you are hearing it on the
radio, none of that matters; it sounds like a prime three minutes of Motörhead
and bodes well for the long-player to follow.

Once the needle hits the groove, the shortcomings are all too apparent:
Lemmy's bass is poorly recorded, the vocals aren't multi-tracked enough to
give the chorus weight and the riff is weaker than expected. Philthy sounds like
he has been recorded in an empty warehouse but clearly puts everything he
has in to, driving the song as fast as he can to give it the illusion of substance.
Coming up with an actual ending to the song appears too difficult, so they
fudge a finale together by fading out on the trailing riff from the chorus.

Thankfully, there are a few excellent live versions available which suggest that
the song is sturdy (although the lyrics could still do with work), and it was the
studio production that caused most of the problems.

'Heart Of Stone' (Clarke/Kilmister/Taylor)

Laughably, one of the working titles of this was 'Lemmy Goes To The Pub', and there was even a full set of lyrics to accompany it. Eddie kept a collection of the mixes and, when he was allegedly short of money, he apparently leased them out to the notoriously bootleg-friendly Receiver Records in the late 1980s.

The final version is an improvement on that early vision but really doesn't add up to much in the end. The lyrics border on cliché, but if it had been attached to a memorable tune or incorporated a particularly classy melody, then the words could have been ignored. As it is, the listener is left with a foreboding that standards are already slipping. As with the title track, simply taking the whole song at tremendous speed (listen out for live versions of the era where Philthy's feet move so fast they are a blur of sound) really doesn't disguise the cracks in the songwriting.

'I'm The Doctor' (Clarke/Kilmister/Taylor)

Even if it had only been at one remove (Philthy's constant visits to casualty), Lemmy had been hearing a lot about doctors. The basic musical thrust of this song is back to rock and roll, while the sonics suggest that we are listening to *Motörhead* or even *On Parole* demos. The Doctor, in this case, seems to be more of a purveyor of illicit chemicals rather than an avuncular GP. Again the cack-handed garage production takes a lot of the strength out of the song, but the tragedy is that this would have been discarded from any other rehearsal session before it even got to the recording stage.

'Go To Hell' (Clarke/Kilmister/Taylor)

Another bitter lyric about a partner doing the protagonist wrong and that they can, therefore, 'go to Hell'. Emphatically neither Shakespeare nor Dylan, it barely rises above the level of barrel-scraping, much like the accompanying music. Eddie actually sounds bored playing the uninspired riff and the guitars appear to have been recorded in a metal shack, such is the bright tone and sharp treble that is exhibited. Again, the band opt for the 'live crescendo' ending, but this time it's the most interesting part of the song and that should be a crime, punishable by hanging the producer upside down until he agrees to the hiring of a real producer.

'Loser' (Clarke/Kilmister/Taylor)

Lemmy finally gets into lyric-writing gear with this self-deprecating tale of a struggling musician-come-good which bangs its chest with male braggadocio and yet ends with a sarcastic comment about the person who called the musician a 'Loser':

Big wide smile gonna bring me down
They don't know their arse from a hole in the ground

Musically a genuine stomp, this has hints of excitement in its thudding pace but again, the production and the guitar tone let it down. The voice, however, is in fine form, even if it is struggling against the thin sound.

'Sex & Outrage' (Clarke/Kilmister/Taylor)
This is another suspect lyric, alluding to teenage groupies, which appears to have been thrown together and again misses the mark when it comes to complementing the music. This is more of a basic thrash in search of a decent riff than a completed tune. Everything here seems half-formed and under-rehearsed as if they were unprepared for recording, so just taped their early exploratory sessions and then chucked first draft lyrics on top. The only outrage here is how poor this number is.

'America' (Clarke/Kilmister/Taylor)
A veteran of touring America (certainly in comparison to his bandmates, who were novices at this stage), Lemmy scatters a series of movie-style lines over the tune, relating his first impressions of the country and, unconsciously, looking with a certain wistfulness at the way it is all new to his bandmates. There is a savage jerking riff to go with the tasteful vocal melody and a rather good chorus to accentuate the words. While not the greatest Motörhead song, it does, at least, pull the album out of the mire of mediocrity that it has degenerated into.

'Shut It Down' (Clarke/Kilmister/Taylor)
The dreadful mess of the vocal recording rears up again here. Lemmy does his best, but it sounds like he is shouting into a wind tunnel this time. There's a sturdy song struggling to get out, but it is absolutely hamstrung by the pathetic production and the risible mix. Actually, the idea of remixing this album is not such a terrible prospect. A redux version could be far stronger than is currently the case and there are fine precedents available.

'Shut It Down' is a brisk gallop through another break-up song. It recycles some of the words that appear on 'Remember Me, I'm Gone', and it even recycles sentiments common to other songs here. The music is fundamentally sound and, if Lemmy were still alive, he could have a better crack at rewriting the words to create a far superior song.

'Speedfreak' (Clarke/Kilmister/Taylor)
There is not even a single entendre here, just a bare-faced proclamation of honesty: the band are speedfreaks and they don't care who knows it. A stirring riff and a nice bass line lend urgency to the charging full tilt rush of the music and everything finally comes together. It is just a terrible shame that Eddie and Will were left in charge of the desk for the recording.

Annoyingly, this passes in a flash (most of the songs present here are only around the three-minute mark) when it could easily have been extended. The music-to-fade-out ending is both a cliché and indicative of the slapdash nature of the whole project.

'(Don't Let 'Em) Grind Ya Down' (Clarke/Kilmister/Taylor)

Lacking any of the nostalgia that could have surfaced, this bad-mouthed look back at the early days of the band is a rallying call of dogged perseverance and, with hindsight, an unexpected work of hubris.

Musically, this has punk written all over it, although the sonic atmosphere is, if anything, poorer than that of The Damned's god-awful *Music For Pleasure* album. The unfortunate Nick Mason, drummer for Pink Floyd,was responsible for that production. Maybe Eddie and Will were taking tips from Nick...

'(Don't Need) Religion' (Clarke/Kilmister/Taylor)

It doesn't take a genius to spot the lyrical slant of this song, but it is a cogent and forceful, repudiation of religion and its practices. Lemmy was obviously aggrieved by something religious on the day he wrote this, and he spells it out, surprisingly, in the first verse:

Don't need no blind belief
Don't need no comic relief
I don't need to see the scars
I don't need Jesus Christ Superstar
Don't need no Sunday television
Bet your life you don't need religion

Boasting a slower, grimier and just plain nastier riff than usual, this comes on like prime heavy metal pub rock with the added joy of a striking backwards guitar solo and a pummelling lurch that points to the future. Strangely addictive, this plodding tune has a depth to it that outshines its brethren in every respect.

'Bang To Rights' (Clarke/Kilmister/Taylor)

Expecting a tale of crime and the Police, this is actually Lemmy in somewhat confessional mode. In three verses, the narrator holds up his hands and says he has been caught fair and square, carrying on with someone else. The protagonist feels a little remorse but mostly expresses annoyance that it might lead to a scene and a public break-up.

Eddie pulls a tasty riff out of his fingers and indulges in a couple of neat solos while the rhythm section pound away. There is even room left for a brief bass solo, but Philthy has no such luck in the limited time available. Ending on a relatively high note, this draws a veil over some of the dross that preceded it.

Related recordings
'Remember Me, I'm Gone' (Clarke/Kilmister/Taylor)

Starting life as 'Same Old Song, I'm Gone', it was relegated to a b-side and benefitted from a rewrite. Lemmy toned down the words of this song of regret as the original lyrics are quite bald:

No, I can't believe it, that I lost you
Coulda had you easy, just didn't come true
Now another boy fills your groin with joy
I was away too long
It's the same old song, I'm gone

Another relationship lost to the road, it seems. The new opening verse puts things a little more obliquely (but not much):

I can't believe it, that I lost you
Could've made it happen, but it didn't come true
Some other guy got you home and dry
Only been the one, same old song
Remember me, I'm gone

Starting with a deliciously overwrought bass, this descends into a charging drum-driven Motortune that has, as is often the case, a real need to be on the parent album.

Stand By Your Man EP

Personnel:
Lemmy Kilmister: vocals, bass
Philthy Animal Taylor: drums
Wendy O Williams: vocals
Richie Stotts: guitars
Wes Beech: rhythm guitar
Produced at Eastern Sound Studios, Toronto, Canada, May 1982 by Lemmy, Rod
Swenson and the musicians.
Did Not Chart
Running time (approximate): 8:36

'Stand By Your Man' (Billy Sherril/Tammy Wynette)

Looking to repeat the success of the HeadGirl collaboration Lemmy hooked
up with wild punk band The Plasmatics and their infamous singer. Lemmy, it
appeared, was infatuated with Wendy O Williams (ex-stripper/ex-performer
in live sex shows who found herself fronting an underground US punk band)
as he saw someone even more extreme than himself. He and Philthy thought
it would be a laugh and that it might repeat the HeadGirl success and were
unwilling to listen to Eddie, who could see a calamity in the offing. Eddie
turned up for the initial EP session and walked out when he heard the first
underwhelming results. He was supposed to be producing the tracks, as well
as playing on them, which led to Plasmatics manager/songwriter Rod Swenson
ostensibly taking over at the last second.

Lemmy, in a provocative mood, then played the rough mix of the song to
Eddie on the tour bus, and until the day he died, Eddie remained angry at the
way this impetuous project temporarily scuppered both of their careers. The
utter mauling of the song starts in the first few seconds of music and continues
through the screeched and wailed vocalising, the barely tuneful chorus and
the ridiculous solo, finally ending up with a caterwauling din that shows
none of the participants in a good light. The sound, last-minute producer
aside, is appalling and barely merits the term demo, never mind finished mix.
The drumming, from the normally reliable Philthy, is lumpy and sounds like
someone is striking the drums with a tightly gripped duvet. The guitars only
pay lip service to being in tune, although it could be argued that this was in the
spirit of punk, where musicians play to the edge of their abilities.

The failure of *Iron Fist* was compounded by this ill-fated folly and it led, in
short order, to Eddie's resignation. The song itself is a blot on Motörhead's
catalogue that will never quite be rubbed out.

'Masterplan' (Richie Stotts/Rod Swenson)

While The Plasmatics popped out a serviceable 'No Class' cover, two-thirds of
Motörhead tackled this throaty rendition of The Plasmatics greatest non-hit.

Eddie is immediately missed both for his playing and for his (admittedly) limited production skills. 'Masterplan' suffers from the same leaden production of its companion, but the sheer force of the song is visible even through all of these inhibitors. Two of the four members of The Plasmatics also play on this session, making it more of a MotorMatic recording rather than a bonafide Motörhead cover. Lemmy gives it maximum cackle (well, he sounds like he is laughing while he is singing), and the rest of the musicians attempt to keep up. It is a worthy b-side, nothing more, although it doesn't fail quite so spectacularly as 'Stand By Your Man'.

Another Perfect Day (Bronze, June 1983)

Personnel:
Lemmy Kilmister: vocals, bass
Brian Robertson: guitars, piano, fender piano, backing vocals
Philthy Animal Taylor: drums
Produced at Olympic and Eel Pie Studios, London, February-March 1983 by Tony Platt.
Highest chart place: UK: 20
Running time (approximate): 44:09

Backed into a corner and forced to postpone the accompanying tour, the hunt was on for a speedy replacement for Eddie. Anvil's Steve 'Lips' Kudlow was approached but declined the offer as Anvil had just released their seminal *Metal On Metal* album and were expecting to hit the big time soon after. Philthy, being a huge Thin Lizzy fan, then suggested contacting Brian Robertson as soon as the gnashing of teeth had settled. Lemmy jumped at the idea and called Brian up for duty. Brian came with a few stipulations and concerns regarding his induction into the band, chief of which was that he couldn't play much of the current repertoire as it was too 'in your face'. Lemmy assured him that they weren't looking for a clone of Eddie but, instead, wanted Brian for what he could bring to their sound. On that basis, Brian agreed and started working on new song material. Even at this stage, there seems to have been a miscommunication as Brian saw himself getting a starring role while Lemmy and Philthy understood that Brian had joined Motörhead, not 'Motörhead featuring Brian Robertson'. Unfortunately, when you are in a hole, no one looks too closely at the contract or the implied fine print. The protracted recordings were the result of Brian's attention to detail and his urge to introduce a greater finesse and a more varied palette of sounds into the mix. Lemmy quickly got fed up with the endless multi-tracked overdubs and the array of effects Brian used, all of which had to go through his pedalboard and took hours to achieve. As it was, the album was greeted with lukewarm reviews and poor sales on release and, far from reviving the band's fortunes, it plotted a significant downward trajectory for the trio.

Time has been kind to this album, although not to Brian Robertson, as, according to Lemmy: 'I love that album, it's just Brian I couldn't fucking stand.'

'Back At The Funny Farm' (Kilmister/Brian Robertson/Taylor)

Even on the first few notes of *Another Perfect Day*, it is obvious that they have benefitted immensely from the reintroduction of a skilled producer. Combined with the attention of a world-class guitarist intent on introducing musicality and dynamism into the sonic soup of Motörhead's previous outings, the sound is at once melodic and very much a progression on Motörhead's innate noise. Lemmy shouts 'top notch' at the beginning (probably talking to the album's engineers but actually identifying the standard of the album), and a whole new era for the band explodes into life.

The lyrics are hardly politically correct as Lemmy pulls out an undoubtedly humorous take on madness, ending with the amusing pay-off verse:

Can't find the windows but I gotta get outside
Can you help me stand, it feels like both my legs have died
What was that injection, 'cos I think it's goin' wrong
I really like this jacket but the sleeves are much too long

You can almost hear Lemmy giggling as he approached the microphone while Brian put down some extraordinary backing vocals for the last chorus. The subtext, of course, is that this is a comic commentary on the new line-up and the ridiculousness of the rock lifestyle.

This melodic yet tough start to this, as it turned out, one-off album, is already endearing and Lemmy takes the time to hone his lyrics for this semi-comeback offering. The rhythm section still produce that signature Motörhead sound while Brian, as promised, adds some subtlety and depth to the guitar amid lashings of six-string overdubs. In many ways, the looser and more melodic guitars sound even more Motörhead than the harshly tinny noise of *Iron Fist*.

'Shine' (Kilmister/Robertson/Taylor)
Astonishingly chosen as the second single, there is an immediate Motörhead crunch to the opening that should, at least, have satisfied casual listeners that all was well in the band's new configuration. Brian produces a casually shining riff and invests the trundling rhythm with a smooth edge that could (if the wind was in the right direction) suggest commercial appeal. Brian works in fender piano, although it is used sparingly, which also adds to the classier sonic palette being constructed here.

The lyrics match the musical backing, although they are a notch down from the opener. Full of male braggadocio, this is another one where Lemmy must have been chortling quietly to himself, especially when he penned the line 'my beauty gonna meet your beast', as this is clearly another use of comedy in his words.

'Dancing On Your Grave' (Kilmister/Robertson/Taylor)
The listener is likely to be startled by the slow chiming guitar introduction when faced with that title, but Lemmy always did like a nice juxtaposition. It has a clear descendant in 'Love Me Forever' (from *1916*), but that doesn't then spring into life with a marvellous hook line, a memorable riff and an almost pop-like tune. Brian throws in a masterly solo to bring the whole thing to an end. The lyric is ostensibly a dig at a partner who has left the narrator and then died later. Actually, under the surface, Lemmy is berating those people who believed Motörhead were finished and should have packed it in when Eddie

left. With glorious 20:20 hindsight, the obvious irony of the opening line was entirely unintentional:

> I know you thought you're a real operator

Arresting and thoroughly likeable, this elevates the calibre of the songs being performed here and it indicates that this trio could have had a fantastic future, circumstance notwithstanding.

'Rock It' (Kilmister/Robertson/Taylor)
This is another of Lemmy's odes to rock and roll as the saviour for both himself and the world. Strapped to an amped-up rock and roll tune, this sees the first use of the piano (courtesy of Brian) on a Motörhead song and, while it may not be innovative or breaking new ground, it has a nice hard rock chug that suits the subject matter.

'One Track Mind' (Kilmister/Robertson/Taylor)
Sometimes lyrics arrive easily, sometimes they are impossible to pull together. Often, writers will use little lessons or aids to help spark their imaginations. In this case, Lemmy seems to have picked up a simple exercise of using numbers that show each verse, e.g., verse two:

> Two lane highway, two hand car
> Two lane highway, too damned far
> Two faced women, two time guys
> Two faced women, two black eyes

Starting with another nice little guitar figure, this kicks off a slow, pounding groove that seems to move like treacle. The words don't really do the music justice, especially as Brian puts a great many tricks into his middle eight solo. He multi-tracks it, he seems to collapse three completely separate ideas into it and he even varies wildly on the speed of his fretwork to provide variety. He really does put everything he has into this album and, whether because of his presence or not, those ultra-clichéd 'live' thrashing-about endings of the past are banished to history.

'Another Perfect Day' (Kilmister/Robertson/Taylor)
Motörhead often start their albums with the title track, but they break with tradition on this occasion and nestle it comfortably in the middle. Written in a somewhat sarcastic tone and sung in a surprisingly monotone croak, Lemmy sings of all the bad things that can happen on a perfect day. Lemmy sells himself short here with a bland set of words that do nothing for the inspired tune underpinning them. Perhaps this is why the title track is buried here, it didn't come out as well as the band hoped and they decided to hide it in the undergrowth of the album.

It has a beautiful blues-rock introduction and it powers along in a mid-paced strut that only needs a memorable chorus to really ignite it.

'Marching Off To War' (Kilmister/Robertson/Taylor)

The theme of war and its pointlessness and profound consequences emerges here. Lemmy lambasts the waste of human life, empathising with the soldiers and their patriotic recruitment and subsequent disillusionment with insight and understanding. From the language used, this is clearly about the First World War and it shows Lemmy's deep knowledge and fascination with the subject.

Meanwhile, the music blasts into life with a galloping tempo that subtly undercuts the lyrics. The jaunty playing of the song may well be highlighting the initial optimism of the soldiers heading to the front, but the words paint an altogether bleaker picture and the music jars rather than complements the lyrical thrust.

'I Got Mine' (Kilmister/Robertson/Taylor)

Releasing this as the first single was a sensible move as it has the Motörhead spirit in abundance and provides a pretty decent stab at a radio-friendly calling card for the album.

Initially, it looks like another relationship song, but the idea is inverted when it turns out that Lemmy is singing of his adoration for rock and roll music and the joy it gives him to both play it and earn a living from it. Well, just about. The band were still sleeping on friends' floors or moving in with a female companion so they could get a bed for the night. While royalties were coming through, they didn't amount to much because a lot of the finance went on the costs of touring and paying off record company debts. Record companies advance a group or solo artist money so that they can afford to record in a studio and pay a producer. They then expect the amount to be paid back from the royalties.

Record companies love a live album as the costs are relatively small and if the records are commercially successful, everybody wins. Motörhead were still waiting for the royalties from *No Sleep 'til Hammersmith* to come through.

'I Got Mine' has a catchy, jangly guitar introduction and the song fits a pop pace while the vocals are mixed a little higher to ensure that people can hear what Lemmy is singing about. Brian again plays a blinder and he really gets to stretch out as the end approaches.

'Tales Of Glory' (Kilmister/Robertson/Taylor)

You might be forgiven for thinking that this is a song about old soldiers and their war stories, but Lemmy again pulls the rug out and uses it as a way to tell a prospective partner that he might not be the settling down kind. He also wants to accentuate his carefree lifestyle. The lyrics finish by berating the person for talking too much:

Endlessly, endlessly
Your mouth won't set me free
Endlessly, endlessly
Rabbit in my ear

This is probably the low point in terms of the words.

There is a distinct whiff of Eddie in the musical backing and Brian seems to fit in rather too well at this point, and the brevity of the song suggests that this has a good dose of punk in its DNA while being unremarkable.

'Die You Bastard!' (Kilmister/Robertson/Taylor)
The same cannot be said for the final track, however, as the music is driving and the lyrics are a little more considered, even if they are somewhat melodramatic. Starting with a loud belch, the band steam into a juddering, stuttering riff that only relaxes when the chorus riff is introduced. The jerky rhythm gives the nightmarish tales of living shadows, vampires and murderous strangers a perfect backdrop, while the shouting of the title as the end approaches has all the bile and rage in it that Lemmy can muster, and that's a lot.

While it isn't outside the band's comfort zone, this finishes a surprisingly virile and musical album with a real crunch.

Related recordings
'Turn You Round Again' (Kilmister/Robertson/Taylor)
Shoved on to a B-side, there's a cracking riff from Brian, a second great riff reserved for the chorus and a freewheeling solo that rounds proceedings off with a flourish.

Meanwhile, Lemmy ruminates on his outsider status and his band's fortunes and comes to terms with these particular demons, saving his little revelation for, as usual, the third verse:

I'm gonna tell you something you must believe
I've got a hat full of jokes, waiting up my sleeve
Forget cancellation, I know the game
It's a different face
But the name's the same

Certainly, while he was writing the lyrics, Lemmy was extremely pleased with Brian and what he had brought to the group.

No Remorse (Bronze, September 1984)

Personnel:
Lemmy Kilmister: vocals, bass
Phil Campbell: guitars
Wurzel [Michael Burston]: guitars
Pete Gill: drums
Produced at Britannia Row Studios, London in May 1984 by Vic Maile.
Highest chart place: UK: 14 (UK)
Running time (approximate): 83:34

Brian was sacked from the band for refusing to play many of the old standards but also because he declined to wear something in keeping with the Motörhead image; on stage, he would frequently appear in pink satin shorts, legwarmers, ballet shoes (so, he claimed, he could literally dance on his effects pedalboard!), a fishnet top and with his short hair held back by a headband, which upset the more conservative fans in the audience.

Lemmy started looking for new blood to fill the vacancy. He was open in his desire to carry on with the band and used the music press to aid his search for new talent, remarking that he would probably end up with a couple of unknowns. No-one, it seems, was more unknown than Wurzel and, when he played in unison with Phil Campbell, they brought back memories of Motörhead's initial twin-guitar pitch. Lemmy was sold to the idea early on and recruited them both in double-quick time. For about three days, everything looked positive again.

Then Philthy left to follow Brian into Operator and Lemmy was staring at the ashes of his band and wondering if he was going to be able to start again. He had two eager and ambitious guitarists waiting in the wings, yet he could have given up. Relying on stubbornness, determination and the unnerving awareness that he had no idea what else he could do except play music, Lemmy began searching for drummers. At the age of 37, he obviously felt he was too stuck in his ways to pursue anything else.

Lemmy knew Pete Gill as a fine drummer for Saxon and someone he thought he could get on with, given the touring both bands had done together. Pete had injured his hand in 1981 and had been forced to depart from Saxon as a result. He was at a loose end when the call came to join Motörhead and he was reportedly delighted at the chance to join.

Bronze, lacking the foresight of all record companies, saw the end of Motörhead approaching with this second loss of a guitarist so, instead of investing in the group by asking for a new album, they opted for a greatest hits compilation from existing sources. Lemmy, cannily, told them he wouldn't endorse the product if he wasn't placed in charge of the project and then he persuaded Bronze that the new four-man line-up must have the opportunity to record some material for the collection as a showcase, resulting in a rushed but productive recording session where six songs were put down. Lemmy rather botched the tracklisting as it features rather too many b-sides, low points and unrepresentative songs, but it is the most useful of the early compilation albums. Bronze went overboard on the packaging once they had received the tapes, and sent the double vinyl album (and even the cassette variant) out into the world sporting a magnificent silver stamped full leather sleeve and then opted for expensive TV advertising. These twin costs are partly responsible for the bankrupting of Bronze because the release sold well and they had to keep manufacturing the costly covers. Record companies are clueless halfwits sometimes.

'Killed By Death' (Michael Burston/Phil Campbell/Pete Gill/ Kilmister)

Appropriating the title from Spike Milligan (Lemmy was a regular radio listener in his earlier years and was a fan of *The Goon Show*), Lemmy gives us his best throaty growl and lets the newly constituted band lay down a punishing backing for this surprisingly slow crawl. Given the usual pace of a Motörhead tune, this sounds as if everyone had just smoked dope before they hit 'record'. The title really sums it up; this is a song about laughing in the face of inevitable death. It proved to be a song that, for some reason, connected with both audiences and Lemmy, who would play it live probably a thousand times and still loved it.

There's a definite Phil vibe to the bedrock riff while Wurzel throws in a great lead guitar figure and Lemmy throws several different vocal mannerisms into the pot to prove he's enjoying himself. Only the drum noise that Pete is saddled with brings the side down as it crashes about in search of a meaner, cleaner sound for the kick drums and cymbals to match the ridiculous lyrics: Lemmy really does sing/say 'killed by a bunch of death' which ought to show he's joking!

'Snaggletooth' (Burston/Campbell/Gill/Kilmister)

The band's Joe Petagno logo is hereby immortalised in song. Well, kind of. Lemmy remarks on the surprising perseverance of his band and then hits the chorus with:

> I'm gonna raise your roof
> Ring your bell and that's the truth
> Speed don't kill and I'm the proof
> Just call me Snaggletooth

... which is where he turns the spotlight on himself and laughs at not being the most handsome of men, but there is no denying his presence and charisma.

The entire band seem to be in a race for the finish line, so fast do they play, but this is definitely a song with a startling Wurzel riff that powers everything forward while both guitarists present battling solos as if they are in a duel.

'Steal Your Face' (Burston/Campbell/Gill/Kilmister)

Lemmy seemed to find inspiration in classic monsters around this time, he has mentioned vampires and werewolves, but now he seems to have struck upon a slow-moving terror that, ultimately, finds you and removes your face. The creature is left unnamed and it's probably scarier that way.

The ultra-fast treble-y guitar introduction is crushed by a bruising thud that steamrollers through the entire song and suggests the band is heading for distinctly heavier territory in their future. A screeching solo outstays its welcome, but the cymbal effects from Pete near the fade out add some much-needed interest to the tune. The song gained a limited live life but was captured for a b-side for the forthcoming 'Deaf Forever' single.

'Locomotive' (Burston/Campbell/Gill/Kilmister)

The train/sex metaphor makes its first appearance here and it proved to be a subject that Lemmy would return to later on. Again the blunt production does the song few favours, although the blazing drum introduction and the sheer ferocious pace of the song pummel the inadequacies into the dust. Lemmy, unfortunately, constantly sounds like his voice is about to crack under the strain, but he does manage to last to the amphetamine-fast rock and roll drenched guitar solo before giving up. Pete shows off his impressive skills, proving he is no slouch at keeping up with, even surpassing, Philthy, but he has little character to exhibit.

'Locomotive' is a partial failure, although it has its admirers for its thrash/speed metal leanings.

Related recordings

'Under The Knife [slow]' (Burston/Campbell/Gill/Kilmister)

Tucked away on the b-side of the 12' single (for 'Killed By Death') were two songs with the same name. Initially, people thought there was a misprint on the sleeve; then the feeling was that the song had been mis-pressed to vinyl twice and finally, punters suggested it was simply twin versions of the same song. Nothing could be further from the truth. Lemmy must have been chortling to himself mightily when he hit upon the wheeze: these are two completely different songs that have two entirely distinct sets of lyrics with only the name to connect them. He had a peculiar sense of humour sometimes. In practice, the only way to differentiate between them is to listen to the tempo, hence the titles given here.

Given the tired riff and perfunctory drumming, this feels like a b-side afterthought, but Lemmy makes a meal of the lyrics to stretch to the end of the song. Another thought on leaving a partner behind due to the touring life, this is not one of his standout lyrics. A single nice solo doesn't make up for the by-the-numbers songcraft, but at least it gives the listener something to latch on to.

'Under The Knife [fast]' (Burston/Campbell/Gill/Kilmister)

Lemmy goes all out with the first draft lyrics, marrying thoughts on hospital surgery to more reflections on the rock and roll lifestyle in a blatant attempt to get to the pub as quickly as he can. The words are basically scribbled on an opened out cigarette packet and then sung moments later:

You ain't gonna feel no pain
Steel needle in your brain
Twisted sister, nurse, it's worse
An' it's only the second verse

On this evidence veteran lyric writers have nothing to worry about. Lemmy is clearly not taking this very seriously as, when the ridiculously played solo really takes hold, he shouts 'mangle it Wurzel!' with undisguised glee at his own pun.

'Under The Knife [fast]' has a far better riff than its opposite number and musically, it stands up as a pretty decent stab at a Motörhead song. The production hampers the tune, but it's a valiant attempt and it could have sat on *No Remorse* with ease, knocking out 'Locomotive' or 'Steal Your Face' in a brutal coup.

'Countdown' (Albert Jarvinen/Kilmister/MakeLaakkonen/P. Puhtila)

Albert Jarvinen Band Recorded: 1984
Found on: Born To Lose – Live To Win: The Best of Lemmy (CD)

In early 1984, quite unsolicited, Lemmy was sent a completed backing track by Finnish fan and seasoned guitarist Albert Jarvinen and was asked to contribute lyrics and vocals to this breezily produced but somewhat forgettable hard rock tune. Lemmy duly obliged with pen and voice and, accidentally, invented the way many of his future collaborations would be achieved. Cheekily it claims that Lemmy was somehow the producer of the whole song, although he only had a hand in recording his own vocals. Musically this is heavy rock of its period but with a flashy guitarist, a bass player who is emphatically not Lemmy and a commercial sheen. Lemmy opts for a spoken gravel-deep-voice intoning 'count down'(yes, he splits it up as two words for some reason) as the ostensible chorus and then sings in a voice soaked in alcohol while throwing in some throat-shredding screams just to punctuate the end of the verses. The tune itself is a little more mannered than equivalent Motörhead songs of the period, but it lacks that crucial hook, whether musical or lyrical, that would have elevated it to the status of lost classic. As it is, it occupies a dusty corner in a little-explored area of Lemmy's discography.

Lemmy would never admit it, but he was humbled by the relative failures of *Iron Fist* and *Another Perfect Day* and the terrible fall-out from his duet with Wendy O Williams, and subsequently used his spare time for extra-curricular collaborations so that Motörhead could move on. The seed of that route forwards was planted here and it served Lemmy well for the remainder of his life, allowing him to separate his solo appearances from his Motörhead duties.

Orgasmatron (GWR, August 1986)

Personnel:
Lemmy Kilmister: vocals, bass
Phil Campbell: guitars
Wurzel: guitars
Pete Gill: drums
Produced at Master Rock Studios, London, May 1986 by Bill Laswell and Jason Corsaro.
Highest chart place: UK: 21
Running time (approximate): 35:36

Touring was the mainstay of Motörhead's life and during 1985, they were billed to appear alongside Hawkwind at an anti-heroin gig, so, inevitably, Lemmy popped up on stage to guest on 'Silver Machine'. A shrewd promoter could virtually guarantee Lemmy's attendance if the two bands were booked on the same day but at different times.

By 1986 Bronze had collapsed and no other record companies were knocking down the door to sign Motörhead. Manager Doug Smith resorted to an old tactic and simply created a label for the band (along with Hawkwind, Girlschool and the reactivated Fastway) to release new songs. GWR Records was the result and they requested an album from their new signing. The budget was tight and the studio time was short (a mere two weeks were set aside for the whole recording), but the band were pointed in the direction of maverick producer Bill Laswell, eclectic purveyor of 'collision music', and they jumped at the chance to work more experimentally. Bill's c.v. bristled with an eccentric array of artists that he had already produced, including Sly and Robbie (the excitingly anarchic dub reggae of *Language Barrier*) and Public Image Ltd. (the remarkable, and still sorely under-rated, classic hard rock *Album*) all before he set to work with Motörhead.

A blinder of a collection, this, unfortunately, came and went with alarming speed from the record-buying consciousness. Lemmy was always forthright in his opinion that *Orgasmatron* was poorly mixed, while Phil derided the production, but they are both wrong; this is an extraordinary use of the studio as an instrument and it remains a firm favourite with fans who enjoy the heavier end of the musical spectrum. Their argument is that the songs bear little relation to rock and roll, and they would be correct. This was a pioneering production, even if there were a few mistakes that crept in because of the stupidly tight schedule; there is talk of harmony/backing vocals going unrecorded for choruses simply as a result of running out of time.

'Deaf Forever' (Burston/Campbell/Gill/Kilmister)
The immediate reaction of most fans on first hearing this opening track was that the band had hired an actual producer for the first time. The guitars grind like heavy metal as never before and the drums clatter, thump and crash in

a locked rhythm as if played by machine. The overall sound is immense and the depth of the sonics is oceanic. A buzzsaw riff is hammered into place by the gigantic drumming that permeates the whole album. A tight snare snaps like a pistol shot, the toms boom and the double bass drum hits like an over-amplified heartbeat. It also features a wonderful solo. Underneath this striking song are the cannibalised remains of the bass line, rhythm and song progression from Hawkwind's 'Master Of The Universe'. This is the song Lemmy has gone on record as wishing he had written, and, in the end, he kind of did! Only, he upped the ampage, hit 'fast forward' on the speed and, inevitably, rewrote the lyrics.

While defiantly commenting on the unfortunate result of playing at maximum volume for a decade (most of the rock musicians from the period are now basically deaf), Lemmy equates the noise to the sounds of ancient Viking battle; swords and shields clashing over the cries of warriors and soldiers fighting and dying. This is a scorcher of an opening song and it sets the scene for the glorious noise that is to follow. As an aside, Lemmy also christens the 2003 box set with his shout of 'Stone Deaf Forever!' near the end of the track.

'Nothing Up My Sleeve' (Burston/Campbell/Gill/Kilmister)

The band tear through this song as if they are releasing all their pent up frustration from the last three years in one supercharged rush. Lemmy barely seems able to catch his breath, and this is in a studio environment, although he does manage to sing as if his vocal cords have recently been sandpapered. It's no great shakes lyrically, a routine tale of a woman doing him wrong but dressed up in the language of magicians, although it has a couple of laugh out loud moments where it's obvious Lemmy is putting in some jokes for himself; the chorus, for example, ends with the line: 'just like that' recalling the catchphrase of well regarded 1970s comedian and magician Tommy Cooper (who literally died on stage during a performance).

Musically this is something else, a collection of stupendous rock and roll riffs bolted to a stripped back chassis of tune and melody. Although blatantly loud, noisy and dripping in sweat, most of the songs here have hummable choruses and catchy hook lines and this is no exception. This is probably the first time that you can hear every gargled syllable of Lemmy's singing and it sounds majestic. Whatever possessed them when they were looking at producers, Bill Laswell somehow managed the almost impossible trick of making Motörhead both heavier metal and more commercial at the same time.

'Ain't My Crime' (Burston/Campbell/Gill/Kilmister)

Here, the riffs collide into each other like dodgems and career off each other as if everyone is playing a different song in the same key while dodging the mad drumming. It is outrageously over-the-top and simultaneously brings a smile to any listener's face. Pete demonstrates his excoriating technique with his pounding rhythm and the guitarists jockey for position in seeing who can outdo the other in the insane riff stakes. Another coruscating joy to hear and another beautiful solo, where the lead guitar just plays chiming chords, merely confirms that this is the comeback to end all comebacks for a band. Lemmy was always firm in his belief that the four-man line-up of Motörhead (regardless of drummer) was his favourite and this album convincingly shows why he might have been correct.

'Claw' (Burston/Campbell/Gill/Kilmister)
Yet more effortlessly juiced up drumming underpins this raging ditty. Beginning with a powerful nod to the double bass drumming of 'Overkill', Pete shows just how strong an engine he can be. The speed is Formula One fast, the guitars recall the sound of cars racing past the pits and the singing is ...well, the singing is debatable, but Lemmy certainly manages to shout and scream in a catchy and almost melodic fashion. There is some sort of backing vocal present here, but it sounds more like the roar of a wounded beast than anything as intelligible as words. With Lemmy close to vocal breakdown by the end, this has all the hallmarks of a studio song destined never to be performed live. This is very unfortunate because it has presence in abundance and it would be an irresistible set closer before the traditional encores finish the night off.

'Mean Machine' (Burston/Campbell/Gill/Kilmister)
A great slavering monster of a track, this has a stunning intertwined twin-guitar opening, a blistering pace, and threatens to overload every single speaker it is attached to – but it is the lovely slide guitar work on the pre-chorus sections that lifts this into the stratosphere. Lemmy gets as close to singing at ridiculous speed as he is able and the guitar solos top off a crazily swift earth-shaker that leaves the listener breathless, never mind the drummer. Given the sheer uninhibited velocity of the song, played by a human being rather than being manipulated by computer or left to a drum machine, the lyrics barely register in comparison, but they are equal to the task and give the impression of relentless driving speed as much as the music. Lemmy slaps a great chorus into proceedings and the whole song sounds like it was designed to accompany stock car racing played on fast forward.

The phrase has a couple of origins: the American football-in-prison film *The Longest Yard* (1974) names their team 'Mean Machine' while the legendary UK comic *2000AD* has a character called Mean Machine, who is a part of the Angel gang, in their best known and longest-running strip *Judge Dredd*. Lemmy could have picked it up from either source.

'Built For Speed' (Burston/Campbell/Gill/Kilmister)
Unusually the band had written this song before the rest of the album was created. It started off as 'On The Road' and was only played in a live situation before it was comprehensively rewritten with a different chorus and other lyrical diversions. Another in a long line of touring songs, the band perhaps

Above: The classic power trio looking hungry both literally (the royalties hadn't started coming through yet) and metaphorically.

Below: A late period promo shot from the final trio, Lemmy looks gaunt and, sadly, on borrowed time.

Left: *Motorhead.* The attention-grabbing graphic design is a classic and remained in place until their demise. (*Chiswick Records*)

Right: *Overkill.* Artist Joe Petagno always wanted to give this cover a 3D effect so that it exploded towards the viewer. (*Bronze*)

Left: *Bomber.* Eddie is in the pilot's position, oddly. The aircraft itself is loosely based on a German Heinkel HE-111 but heavily stylised. (*Bronze*)

Right: *Ace Of Spades* Ahh, the sand pit in High Barton which allowed Philthy to live out his outlaw cowboy fantasy. (*Bronze*)

Left: *Head Girl EP* This time the band updated their plundering of American mythology with gangsters and molls, although they are *all* armed. (*Bronze*)

Right: *No Sleep 'Til Hammersmith* A stunning photo of the iconic bomber lighting rig in action and the only live Motorhead album you really need. (*Bronze*)

Left: A windswept and chiseled Fast Eddie enjoying a moment in the spotlight for the 'Bomber' video.

Right: Philthy is concentrating hard. Less windswept than his colleague, more hedge backwards. It's that 'Bomber' video again.

Left: Lemmy self-advertising, with his microphone prominently placed in that curious position he so adored.

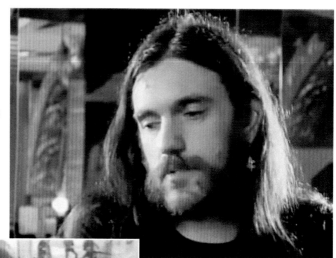

Right: Lemmy denying Motorhead's NWOBHM classification in 1982.

Left: Fast Eddie surrounded by vinyl stock while being interviewed in 1981 for Canadian TV.

Right: Poor Philthy, in the same interview, looking as if his pint has just been snatched away.

Left: *Iron Fist.* The damp faux velvet fist of the album inside the iron glove of the cover. Never was a metaphor so disappointingly reversed. (*Bronze*)

Right: *Stand By Your Man EP.* The band-destroying EP that mentions neither Fast Eddie nor Motorhead on the cover. (*Bronze*)

Left: *Another Perfect Day.* Another perfect Petagno cover, illustrating in graphic form the chaos and turmoil that surrounded its creation. (*Bronze*)

Right: *No Remorse.* Virtually recycling the debut image, but this time the cover was initially clad in real leather. (*Bronze*)

Left: *Orgasmatron.* A joyously ridiculous picture, it was painted for the original album title: *Built For Speed.* (*GWR Records*)

Right: *Rock 'n' Roll* Snaggletooth depicted as a Demon King of Hell. Unfortunately, the music contained within suggests he is the Head of Accountancy. (*GWR Records*)

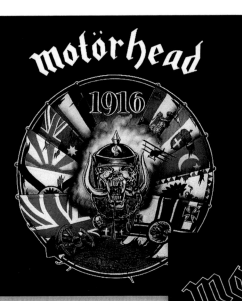

Left: *1916.* The cover mistakenly omitted the French, Bulgarian, Russian, Serbian and Portuguese flags. It always rankled Lemmy. (*WTG/Epic/Sony*)

Right: *March Or Die.* The somewhat amateurish picture is unconsciously indicative of the music contained within. (*WTG/Epic/Sony*)

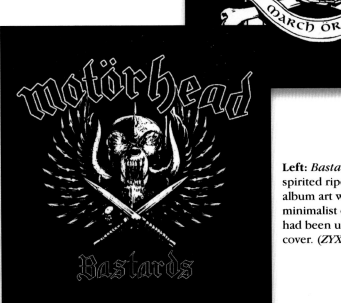

Left: *Bastards.* Petagno's spirited riposte to the previous album art was this bravely minimalist concoction which had been used as a fanzine cover. (*ZYX Music*)

Right: *Sacrifice.* Petagno appears to be channelling Hieronymus Bosch through his own unique filter. The penis tongue caused controversy, unsurprisingly. (*CBH/SPV*)

Left: *Overnight Sensation.* A rare photographic cover: Mikkey is unrecognizable, Phil is an anti-smoking advert and Lemmy ... has no facial hair! (*CBH/SPV*)

Right: *Snake Bite Love.* An almost clichéd concentrate of a heavy metal cover disguises the poor material on offer within. (*CBH/SPV*)

Left: 1987's *Eat The Rich* video followed one of Lemmy's many film appearances. He cuts a commanding figure here.

Right: Phil in younger days, apparently concentrating on his fingering ...

Left: Wurzel, named after the children's book character Worzel Gummidge, looking scruffy enough to earn his nickname.

Right: Philthy looking far too solemn, from the *Eat the Rich* promo.

Left: A somewhat classic pose, during the period of the four-man line-up. Wurzel was a dizzying firecracker on stage.

Right: Lemmy, looking to the heavens and noticing a ghostly interloper. Or a drunken roadie caught in the rigging.

Left: *We Are Motorhead.* Another striking anti-war image, this time recalling WWI advances by the German army. (*SPV*)

Right: *Hammered.* This beautifully rendered golden brooch design has a few easter eggs in the mix. (*SPV*)

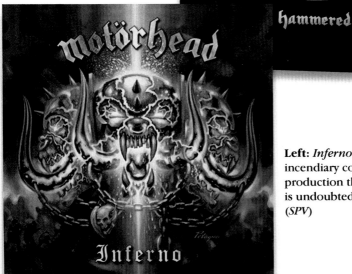

Left: *Inferno* Reflecting the incendiary contents and heavier production this explosive cover is undoubtedly eye-catching. (*SPV*)

Right: *Kiss Of Death.* Looking almost penciled, this detailed cover has a darker tone. This was, sadly, Joe Petagno's last cover illustration. (*SPV*)

Left: *Motorizer.* Surprisingly, the first shield design. English Lions = Lemmy, Snaggletooth = Motorhead, Swedish Crowns = Mikkey, Welsh Dragon = Phil. (*SPV*)

Right: *The World Is Yours.* A great album with a complex cover that doesn't quite work at CD or Download size. (*Motorhead Music/UDR*)

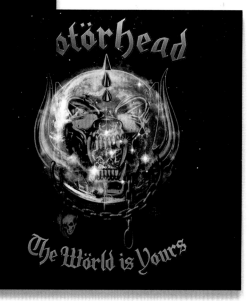

Above: The 'Whorehouse Blues' promo: ostensibly backstage but, obviously, filmed.

Below: A moody black and white shot from the same promo. Is Lemmy really singing into his hand or is that a harmonica?

Above: More 'Whorehouse Blues' shenanigans. Pictured right is Meldrum singer Moa Holmsten. Lemmy guested on their album *Blowin' Up The Machine*.

Below: That increasingly old acoustic blues trio in action for the video shoot.

Left: Head Cat: *Walk the Walk... Talk the Talk*. Duck-walking, brothel creeper-wearing, quiff-bearing, early rock and roller reincarnated. Or a Slim Jim Phantom caricature. (*Niji Entertainment*)

Right: *Aftershock*. A WWII desert scene that revels in its tank imagery and boasts a still virile Snaggletooth. (*Motorhead Music/UDR*)

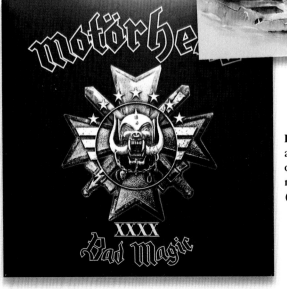

Left: *Bad Magic*. For the 40th anniversary record the band opts for a tarnished silver star motif as a battle medal. Historic. (*Motorhead Music/UDR*)

felt that the words and chorus weren't strong enough to place on the album, but, more than likely, the producer spotted this under-achieving demo and requested a rethink. Sometimes you can hear what a producer actually does.

A lot of the lyrics cover road life, although the third verse is more about the live experience while simultaneously referencing both the endless driving and the ubiquitous amphetamines that were such a part of the band's standard kit. The slower pace of the music emphasises the impression of trucks thundering through the night to the next venue.

When people listen to music nowadays, it is likely to come via a digital form of one sort or another. What many people don't hear now is the gaps between songs on an album. Many digital applications add a pause, whether one is intended or not. If you listen to *Orgasmatron* as a single piece of music (say, from a CD), you will notice that Motörhead have cut the gaps on this album to virtually nothing. This is a conscious mastering choice to ensure it flows together until you get to the title track.

'Ridin' With The Driver' (Burston/Campbell/Gill/Kilmister)

Originally, this was going to be the title of the album, which explains the ferocious locomotive on the cover, and that gives a good indication of the lyrical content of the song. While I don't think Lemmy could ever be accused of being a trainspotter, this is, probably uniquely, a song about railways rather than a metaphor for sex. No doubt it can be read that way, but Lemmy makes frequent use of train vernacular, although the locomotive itself is called the Thunderchief (after the American F-105 single-seat combat aircraft), and continues using the language of the railways of the 1940s and 1950s.

Pete throws out a punishing drumming pace, thrashing his kit as if he were in a fiercely savage fight for his life, while the remaining trio dash for the finish line. The ear-splitting squalling solo deserves mention for simply being one of the most uncomfortable sounds ever to be emitted into the atmosphere, suiting the thrust of the song in every way. Nevertheless, this stands up as another impressive song on an album bursting with almost superhuman vitality.

'Doctor Rock' (Burston/Campbell/Gill/Kilmister)

Charging straight into the heart of the song and, incidentally, carrying on with his lyrical Doctor fixation, Lemmy muses (admittedly quite loudly) on the health benefits of his lifestyle and then ends by praising groupies. He chucks in a sublime chorus and a two-speed verse/chorus structure which, astonishingly, appears to have a shuffle beat under the chorus before it speeds up into the verses again. Lemmy gets an extremely unexpected bass solo and even manages to slide the lines:

Chin up, shoulders back
You've got a body like a Marshall stack

... into proceedings before tearing off into the ionosphere with the chorus again.

Unlike virtually every other album, there is no fat visible here; the songs are pared to the bone and take up no more space than they need, there's barely any gristle here too; perhaps a couple of solos that don't quite work and maybe a song that doesn't achieve the heights of the others. The cruelty is that this album wasn't recognised as a masterclass at the time.

'Orgasmatron' (Burston/Campbell/Gill/Kilmister)

Saving the most momentous until last, Lemmy brings his hidden poetic soul to the fore, coupled with a swirling and mesmeric miasma of multi-tracked guitars that fades in like an approaching sandstorm. The music betrays his psychedelic roots, but the band give it a switch-blade sharpness that reeks of anger and vengeance. It slows the pace to a broken glass crawl, drenches the number in feedback and drawkcab guitar and emits a riff haze that swamps the soundscape, all the while clamped to the huge sounding drums and the gravelly vocals.

When it was played live, it was visually captivating as Lemmy stood, head back, bathed in a sickly green spotlight. It shone down on him as he recited three verses of poetry:

>...It refers to the three things that I hate most in life – organised religion, politics and war.

... and each subject gets a verse of its own. So pleased was he, with his lyrics, Lemmy insisted that the entire poem was placed centre stage on the rear sleeve of the original album. On a 12' piece of cardboard, it had no choice but to stand out.

The lyrics were written when Lemmy caught them in a dream. He apparently made himself wake up and then wrote them down in ten minutes before going back to bed, forgetting he had scribbled the words down. Now, Lemmy is notorious for self-mythologising (and also very tongue-in-cheek), so his claims might not be entirely accurate, but the end result is, by his own admission, his favourite lyric.

He may have been fermenting the words for some time, given his background in Hawkwind. He was a major participant on 1973's *Space Ritual* and played on the otherwise unreleased 'Orgone Accumulator', which concerned a machine that was purportedly able to collect universal energy from people having sex within it, either singly or as a couple. The same machine, renamed the 'Orgasmatron', is also amusingly referenced in Woody Allen's film 'Sleeper' (1973). Lemmy obviously pondered on the idea for many years before he then radically altered the central conceit to ensure the lyrical thrust was demonstrably different to that of Robert Calvert's original. Lemmy, unusually for him, built the analogy that all three states have an orgasmic purpose for those in command. He could have been forgiven if he had just written another song about a machine that collects sexual energy, but this is a far more thought-provoking and philosophical treatise than that. Mind you, that's not to say he would never write another song about sex...

The combination of psychedelic metal and profound poetry is not to everyone's taste, but no one denies its power or the committed way in which Lemmy delivers the vocal. There are even examples of Lemmy simply reciting the piece as poetry.

The song was re-recorded in 2000 by the longest-lasting trio, and it was only released as an internet download. It is a pale imitation of the original, starting with a simple cymbal crash and then introducing the basic drum beat. The absence of guitars is astonishing, although they come in as the song progresses. All three players seem strangely bored by the experience and the only intriguing variation comes near the end where everything, including the vocals, are put in reverse and the whole atmosphere steps up a notch as it becomes disquieting and uncomfortable listening rather than dull and formulaic.

Rock 'N' Roll (GWR, September 1987)

Personnel:
Lemmy Kilmister: vocals, bass
Phil Campbell: guitars
Wurzel: guitars
Philthy Animal Taylor: drums
The Anadin Brothers: female backing vocals
Michael Palin: spoken word
Produced at Master Rock and Redwood Studios, London, June 1987 by Guy
Bidmead and Motörhead.
Highest chart place: UK: 34
Running time (approximate): 33:56

Touring continued to be the group's default activity and they attacked it with
their usual verve. Philthy, smarting from the abject failure of Operator, asked
Lemmy if he could come back and, perhaps against his better judgement,
Lemmy acceded. This did, however, lend a further degree of credibility to the
ongoing four-man line-up. As the time came to record a follow-up to the unjustly
ignored *Orgasmatron,* the band again found themselves with a ludicrously short
deadline which involved virtually writing, rehearsing and recording the songs at
the same time. Saddled with GWR in-house producer Guy Bidmead they made
the best of a bad situation, but the end result was a record that nobody liked
and, in this case, really was poorly mixed and badly produced.

'Rock'N'Roll' (Burston/Campbell/Kilmister/Taylor)

It is a huge mistake to believe that all lyrics are autobiographical but, with
Lemmy, the line can sometimes be blurred beyond recognition (much like your
eyesight after a night out with him). In this case, however, it seems as if he has
written his eventual epitaph 28 years too early:

> I'm in love with rock'n'roll, it satisfies my soul
> That's how it has to be, I won't get mad
> I got rock'n'roll, to save me from the cold
> And if that's all there is, it ain't so bad
> Rock'n'roll

The newly reinstalled Philthy opens proceedings with a lightweight 'Overkill'
reminder before the serrated guitars kick in. Part of the blame for the poor
performances captured here can be laid at the door of the rotten production,
but some of it must be down to Philthy, who seems to be going through the
motions. Just compare this to Pete's drumming on the previous two releases to
hear the difference.

Heard as a whole, this is a likeable and serviceable song, one that contains a
halfway memorable chorus and that should have become a live staple, but the

tight deadline and the lack of a competent producer left this tune with gaping holes in its structure and it was quickly abandoned like an unruly child.

'Eat The Rich' (Burston/Campbell/Kilmister/Taylor)

Surprisingly leftover from the previous album sessions,this was remixed (or, more accurately, demixed and then ruined) for use in the Comic Strip film soundtrack of the same name. Sonically it matches the rehearsal room ambience of the rest of this album, but it comes to something when a decent recording has to be roughed up so much that it sounds like a ham-fisted demo. It's also worth noting that, as Pete doesn't get a credit, Philthy has probably re-recorded the drums for this tune, echoing his decade-old job for *On Parole*.

Reflecting the darkly comic tone of the film, the lyrics basically concern the unwitting descent into cannibalism of a group of wealthy restaurant attendees. Neither the film nor the song is scalpel-sharp enough to be called a satirical success, but the thought is there. Lemmy certainly relishes every word that he utters, but he is let down by the backing. Musically this has a somewhat fractured beat and some odd-sounding guitar interruptions, which make it a surprising choice for the single release, except that it was tied to the movie to give it a better chance of success.

'Blackheart' (Burston/Campbell/Kilmister/Taylor)

Surprisingly melodic songs pepper this album and this is a prime example. Lemmy's bass is upfront and the guitars toil away at the riffs, and the end result is something catchy and arresting. The lyrics bear all the hallmarks of a late-night target that has already passed and suggest that the narrator is a bad man and prospective partners should be aware of that.

While Motörhead were in the studio, psychedelic glam rock one-hit wonders Dr & the Medics were recording their second album next door, complete with their backing singers. Motörhead felt they needed a certain sweetness added to the chorus, so they persuaded the Anadin Brothers (Wendy and Collette) to add some background vocals, which, as it turned out, were almost entirely buried in the mix.

'Stone Deaf In The USA' (Burston/Campbell/Kilmister/Taylor)

Lemmy gets to introduce the new members of the band to the delights of touring America and virtually predicts his Stateside move in the first verse:

Crossed the ocean in a silver bird, flying into another world
Flying down the Pacific coast, flying up in a silver ghost
Love to be back in Los Angeles
L.A.X. what a sight to see
Stone fox women, crazy days
Table hopping at the Rainbow, babe

The opening riff catches the attention and the urgent loping bass drum beat drives the tune forward while Lemmy sings the melodic chorus with verve. The most striking element is the wonderful slide guitar work from Wurzel that finishes the song with a degree of hope for the rest of the album.

'Blessing' (Michael Palin)

This is a hilarious bonus that only happened because Michael co-owned the studio at this point and Monty Python had recorded several albums there. He was invited along by the band, and their studio engineer. He was then asked to improvise something on the spot and this sweet comedy sketch is the result. It even bears repeated listens. On the day, Michael turned up in full cricket whites and was welcomed as only a hero can be. Lemmy was heard to say: 'It's nice to meet a hero who doesn't turn out to be a cunt.' No one can say fairer than that.

'The Wolf' (Burston/Campbell/Kilmister/Taylor)

The bargain-basement sound effects album has been put to use here. There's a terrible 'howling wind' beginning before an obviously faked wolf howl is thrown at the listener. They may have had a comedy sketch just a moment before, but it's not the time to make the band a laughing stock. Adding in a bit of riff recycling and clichéd chest-beating only brings this song down further. There seems no sign of any inspiration at all here.

Underneath all this nonsense, there is a fantastic Wurzel riff, but it seems to have been lost in the undergrowth of the tune. Even the melody is disappointing. Given more time, the band would have undoubtedly shelved this monstrosity and reworked it into something else. This seems to be the very epitome of something full of sound and fury (they all take this song at a tremendous pace), ultimately signifying nothing. That riff deserved so much better.

'Traitor' (Burston/Campbell/Kilmister/Taylor)

A scything riff and a vengeful lyric still don't add up to much in this further disappointment. Amazingly this song had a long live life and that must be due to the vocals and lyrics, which spit venom and bile at those who have betrayed the band (managers and record companies), and the country (politicians are in for another tongue lashing). There's an interminable repetition of the choppy main riff to end with, which pretty much sums up the whole sorry tune. Intent on giving the world a rock and roll album, the finished record is more like a collection of Motörhead wannabes falling at the first hurdle rather than an indication of the feral live machine they had become.

'Dogs' (Burston/Campbell/Kilmister/Taylor)

Nothing can disguise the indignity that afflicts this jerky if tuneful, song: someone has added pre-recorded handclaps to introduce the third verse. You can almost hear when someone presses 'play' on the handclaps, so sonically aberrant is it. It's the final sign of desperation and it illustrates the total lack of imagination that was behind the control desk for these tunes. Poor Lemmy works hard with the vocals, but he is unable to pull this one out of the mire. Eddie would have given up in disgust.

'All For You' (Burston/Campbell/Kilmister/Taylor)

Over a riff like a blunt razor blade, Lemmy weaves an oddly touching tale of love and romance where he looks back, nostalgically, at his first serious relationship in the late 1960s. Possibly reluctantly, but certainly directly, he bares his heart and acknowledges his emotions. There are some painful truths here:

> We were doomed, babe
> Too much too soon, babe
> Acting like fools

Lemmy is singing about Sue, the girlfriend who died from a heroin overdose, and he doesn't just mean that they were too young; they were 'too soon' because he was white and she was black and, given the racist climate of the time, he was always worried that they were 'doomed'. For a bright and breezy semi-pop song (or as close as Motörhead ever got), the lyrics are both honest and wistful, which is something else that rarely occurs in their catalogue of songs.

Burying it near the end of the album doesn't hide this tuneful love story and, perhaps because there is no need to play like dervishes or posture like macho idiots, the production shortfalls can be ignored. This is, as near as dammit, a commercially-minded rock song with a decent chorus and some nice backing vocals added to the mix (surely a second appearance for the Anadin Brothers) that could have made a great single for someone else.

'Boogeyman' (Burston/Campbell/Kilmister/Taylor)

The end of the album approaches and, barring the upswing of the previous track, there's little hope that this will turn out to be a barnstormer. A murky bass rumble starts things off, then a slicing guitar riff horns in and finally, the shouting begins. Trying to simultaneously combine the night terrors of the bogey man with the idea that no one can boogie with him is a non-starter lyrically. The unlikely inspiration for these words is 'I'm Your Boogieman', a 1976 song by KC and the Sunshine Band, a big hit at the time and one that illustrates Lemmy's wider-ranging musical tastes than was acknowledged. The only saving grace for this Motörhead tune is the earworm catchiness of the guitar riff and the welcome brevity of the song itself.

Related recordings
'Cradle To The Grave' (Burston/Campbell/Kilmister/Taylor)

Disappointingly reminiscent of its parent album, this actually has a worse production sound than that: the drums sound like biscuit tins, the guitar work is of rehearsal standard and the solos are heavy-metal-by-numbers. This is unfortunate as Lemmy is on one of his hobby horses again and stakes a great claim for this new anti-heroin song. It genuinely sounds like it was recorded in one take as a b-side, but Lemmy worked so hard on the words that he put the vocals down anyway.

'Just 'Cos You Got The Power (That Don't Mean You Got The Right)' (Burston/Campbell/Kilmister/Taylor)

This is a highly charged political song from Lemmy's pen that slows the speed to highlight the message. Musically Motörhead opt for a sort-of slow-burning blues, full of resentment and righteous anger, while lyrically, Lemmy goes to town. The longest song Motörhead ever put down on tape, the production deficiencies are less visible here as the sheer force of the tune and the scorching content are more important than the sonic inadequacies of the recording. It all gets set out in the first verse:

You might be a financial wizard, with a sack of loot
But all I see is a slimy lizard with an expensive suit
Go on and run your corporation, go on and kiss some ass
You can buy up half the nation, but you can't buy class
You bastards think it's funny, lying and stealing all your life
Think all there is, is money, got your future wrapped up tight
But Just 'Cos You Got The Power, that don't mean you got the right

This was a regular in live sets for many years, mainly because the entire group loved it and happily kept playing it. It harked back to the blues-rock ancestors of Motörhead and it also gave them all time for a breather, something they all needed as lifelong smokers.

There are worse albums in the Motörhead catalogue, but there aren't many. *Rock 'N' Roll* is an acquired taste and very much a letdown, but it does have a couple of redeeming songs to its credit.

Treading Water

Although their commercial profile was considerably lower in the music-buying world, Motörhead's infamy had spread throughout a large part of the world by this point. There is a joke in the opening season of science fiction comedy *Red Dwarf* (1988) that relies entirely on the recognition of the band's name: pedantic and pompous Arnold Rimmer tells slob (and last human being alive) Dave Lister that he dislikes Lister playing along to the sounds of Rastabilly Skank (a wholly made-up band/genre of music from the 22nd Century) and suggests that Lister listens to 'something classical, like Mozart, Mendelssohn or Motörhead.' It is inspiring to know that the band will be remembered over three million years in the future. Now that's longevity!

The band found that they were treading water again as their record company was unable to provide enough support to pay for more studio time to record another album. A compromise was reached and a stop-gap live album was hurriedly pushed out into the world, but after the commercial failure of *No Sleep At All* in 1988, a sense of dissatisfaction set in. Lemmy, normally one to adopt the ostrich position, quietly began looking for new representation. Phil Carson was an Englishman and an industry heavyweight (his clients had included Led Zeppelin, Yes and AC/DC and he was currently working with Robert Plant, Jimmy Page, Bad Company and Foreigner) who studied the band's situation and, although entirely legal, noted the conflict of interests that could arise when your management is also your record label.

Motörhead were in flux at this time but, sensing that the future looked a little brighter, Lemmy cooked up a few songs along the way to their next album. One of them even found itself premiered on the late-night Channel 4 *Club X* TV programme in 1989:

'Black Leather Jacket' (Kilmister)

Lemmy and the Upsetters. Found on: Stone Deaf Forever! (CD box set)

Almost in spite of himself, Lemmy couldn't resist the pull of a song commission. He was asked if he had a song that could be used for a proposed Channel 4 documentary about, oddly enough, the black leather jacket, based on old mate Mick Farren's book of the same name. Rather than re-tool an old song, the idea grabbed hold of Lemmy and he wrote this in about a day and taught it to the band (and the other musicians) for the live appearance. Bizarrely featuring a unique television line-up of Lemmy on vocals and piano (!), Phil on guitars, Philthy on drums and, amazingly, Eddie playing bass, it was all topped off with a trio of saxophonists hired for the occasion. They were billed as Lemmy and the Upsetters, but this was practically Motörhead concentrate given the talent on show. This song is a fascinating aberration with the piano and saxophones prominent, recalling the beloved rock and roll/R&B bands of Lemmy's youth and it sounds utterly authentic. There is an obvious tip of the (Confederate) hat to *The Blues Brothers* film, which this song would have fitted like a record sleeve and there's a Jerry Lee Lewis vibe that won't be denied. Criminally under-exposed, this remarkable homage to the past would have sat brilliantly with its wide-ranging and experimental neighbours on *1916*, but it was not to be.

After their brief foray into the world of twilight softcore television, Motörhead had to get back to the task in hand: disengaging themselves from their management and recording contract with Doug Smith and signing up with Phil Carson. Phil had contacts throughout the world and suggested that, in order to seal a major label deal, Lemmy might have to move to America (specifically Los Angeles). Lemmy had been thinking of relocating anyway as he felt England was no longer as supportive of the band as they had been and he wanted to make a fresh start. The two things coincided beautifully and Lemmy left Phil to sort out his new accommodation ('it's got to be within walking distance of the Rainbow') and the major record deal. Phil delivered on both, getting a rent-controlled two-bedroom apartment a couple of blocks away from the Rainbow and organising a contract with Sony Music, practically the biggest label in the world at that time.

Before his move to America, Lemmy was asked to contribute an Elvis cover to a charity album entitled *The Last Temptation of Elvis*. It was the germ of a sideline that eventually grew into the HeadCat and a parallel musical career.

'Blue Suede Shoes' (Carl Perkins)
Lemmy and the Upsetters with Mick Green. Recorded: 1990. Found on: Lemmy: Damage Case (CD)
Billed, again, as Lemmy and The Upsetters (this time featuring Mick Green), they were a completely different line-up to the previous incarnation. Mick was one of the guitarists of firm Lemmy favourites Johnny Kidd and the Pirates, an early rock and roll group who got together in the late 1950s and were, for a time, huge stars. Hiring a studio for a couple of days in 1990, they set to work, pouring out a weighty but insistent cover that paid homage to the original but sounded up-to-date and impressive. When the album compilers heard the version, they were so pleased with the result they immediately opted to put the song out as the lead single. Lemmy and Mick were understandably delighted at this reaction and made tentative plans to work together again.

'Paradise' (Mick Green/Kilmister)
Lemmy and the Upsetters with Mick Green. Recorded: 1990. Found on: Lemmy: Damage Case (CD)
Fearing that the single would simply be backed with another track from the album, Lemmy and Mick quickly wrote and recorded their very own b-side, a slower-paced piece of music but in keeping with the Elvis vibe they had tapped into. Echoing a host of more laid-back rock and roll tunes, 'Paradise' was

somewhat of an also-ran in the Elvis tribute stakes, but, hell, this was a b-side and they were enjoying themselves immensely. After the initial excitement, though, the single disappeared (although the album did well enough), and both men returned to their musical day jobs.

1916 (WTG/Epic/Sony, February 1991)

Personnel:
Lemmy Kilmister: vocals, bass
Phil Campbell: guitars
Wurzel: guitars
Philthy Animal Taylor: drums
James Hoskins: cello
Produced at Music Grinder Studios and American Recorders, Los Angeles,
September-November 1990 by Peter Solleyand Ed Stasium.
Highest chart place: UK: 24
Running time (approximate): 39:28

Motörhead toured again and Lemmy kept his hand in writing lyrics for
Girlschool and Lita Ford. Having moved to Los Angeles in the middle of
1990, Lemmy summoned the band for recording sessions in his new home
town and was pleased to discover that, for once, they had a good recording
budget, a renowned producer and a longer time booked into the studio. They
could afford to work hard on their new songs and they were finally looking
forward to a major label release and all the support that entailed (advertising,
videos, music spots on major TV networks, etc.). After close to a four-year gap,
Motörhead eventually put out a studio album of all-new material.

1916 was both a critical and commercial renaissance for the band and they
were ecstatic with the results (a Grammy award nomination, sold-out tours,
major label backing and a brace of genuinely excellent songs).

'The One To Sing The Blues' (Burston/Campbell/Kilmister/Taylor)

In what would quickly become a cliché, but here sounds fresh and invigorating,
Philthy again batters speakers with a drum pummelling that hints at 'Overkill'
but exhibits more melody and a very different style to the older songs. While
Philthy had his faults, he plays up a storm on this album and reminds everyone
listening that he is still a drummer to be reckoned with.

A sharp riff is quickly added to the mix and it's already clear that this is a
quantum leap forward in both sound and sonics. Singing a slightly regretful
tale of another-one-that-got-away, Lemmy uses his voice well and seasons
the lyrics with some nicely self-deprecating lines. There is a joyous feel that
cannot be hidden by the words and, thankfully, everything is starting to sound
effortless again. They were rewarded with a solid opening song and one that
was deemed impressive enough to warrant a single release.

'I'm So Bad (Baby I Don't Care)' (Burston/Campbell/Kilmister/Taylor)

Lemmy is in ebullient mood with his tongue firmly in his cheek on these lyrics.
The first verse sets the tone in style:

I make love to mountain lions
Sleep on red-hot branding irons
When I walk the roadway shakes
Bed's a mess of rattlesnakes

... and it carries on from there. Set against a speeding yet jerky rhythm, it's clear the band are already enjoying themselves as they power through this delightful ditty. Producer Peter Solley makes his mark here by backing up the lyric:

Wham bam thank you Ma'am
Thought I heard the back door slam

... by adding in the very sound mentioned. It sounds right, where the handclaps of 1987 sounded so entirely wrong. If anyone should take these words seriously, they cannot claim to have a sense of humour (honestly, 'I make love to mountain lions'?!). The only word that seems to fit the album so far is exuberance.

'No Voices In The Sky' (Burston/Campbell/Kilmister/Taylor)

Ed Stasium was renowned for his work with the Ramones, which is what attracted Motörhead to him in the first place, and he was originally to produce the entire album. His C.V. was rather more eclectic than that, however, as he was also responsible for several early Talking Heads releases and really made a splash with his production for Living Colour's first two releases, neither of whom are no-nonsense rock and roll bands. Ed gives the song a melodically commercial sheen and accentuates the catchy chorus, but this remains more of an album track than a single. Musically this is a cantering rock and roll tune with a little more crunch in the guitars and a lot more volume (the way the band like it). The steady riff carries on throughout and allows room for a couple of nice solos to be scattered over the top.

Lyrically, Lemmy comes back to a favourite subject: religion and the way its offer of ending up in Heaven is a poor substitute for behaving well on Earth. He spits out a couple of bitter verses and ends the song on a devastating final line:

The ones who dedicate the flags to make you brave
They also consecrate the headstone on your grave
Ritual remembrance when no one knows your name
Don't help a single widow learn to fight the pain

Politicians kissing babies for good luck
TV preachers sell salvation for a buck
You don't need no golden cross to tell you wrong from right
The world's worst murderers were those who saw the light

If the Devil has all the best tunes, he certainly slipped Motörhead a corker in this instance. It must have given Lemmy a huge grin at the thought.

'Going To Brazil' (Burston/Campbell/Kilmister/Taylor)

This is nothing more, nor less, than a catchy R & B song complete with boogie-woogie piano, crazy chorus and kitchen sink production from Ed that glorifies this fun '50s homage. Ironically, this song is apparently the reason he was fired from the *1916* project, as Lemmy discovered Ed had been secretly adding musical parts to the backing track (what he says he heard were claves and tambourines). The idea that tambourines were the straw that snapped the band's patience is an interesting one, given the somewhat experimental and innovative music that would end up on the disc.

For their long-suffering road crew, there is another doff of Lemmy's trusty hat with the snappy verse:

Steve, Clem, Hobbsy,
John, Crazy Dil and Pappy
Had to travel second class
They ain't too fucking happy

With four cracking tunes under their belts, the seeds of musical change were about to bear significant fruit.

'Nightmare/The Dreamtime' (Burston/Campbell/Kilmister/Taylor)

Hinting at the opening to 'Orgasmatron', this begins with swirling drawkcab guitars and vocals before the signature bass kicks in at a slow tempo. The sound of synthesizers providing melodic support is a shock, particularly as the guitars are used for colour rather than throbbing away at a riff. The riff is held by the bass and a submerged beat from Philthy. This is about as far away from rock and roll as Motörhead got. The sound of Lemmy's semi-spoken growled vocals, played in reverse, are extremely unsettling and illustrate the lyrical subject matter well.

The Dreamtime is an Australian aboriginal concept that roughly translates as the ancestral afterlife, although Lemmy uses it as another flavour of Hell in this instance.

'Love Me Forever' (Burston/Campbell/Kilmister/Taylor)

The plaintive electric guitar opening from Phil has cliché written all over it, mostly because it is over-familiar as it has been used by many other bands before. Lemmy was very taken by the riff, but this is second-tier stuff that deserved to be dropped at the rehearsal stage. This is the first real appearance of the rock ballad form on a Motörhead album and it would, unfortunately, not be the last. The lyrics are a little more disturbing than the title implies (one of the lines is: 'faith unto death or a knife in the eye'), which gives the song a punch, but the music is power ballad poor. It follows the classic pattern of quiet verses followed by crashing choruses, and the inevitable emotive guitar solo is by-the-numbers and banal in the extreme. The solo that leads to the graceless finale is, at least, rather more powerful for being restrained.

The third of Ed's trio of songs, this is undoubtedly the most disappointing. Probably the only song on *1916* that doesn't stand repeated listens; it has had a surprising afterlife with two cover versions being recorded. The most interesting recording of which was by veteran German heavy metal singer Doro with whom Lemmy performs a full duet on her 2000 album *Calling The Wild*. The tune and lyrics were unaltered, but the song actually makes more sense as a duet as the words are from both sides of a fractured but loving relationship.

'Angel City' (Kilmister)

Newly ensconced in Los Angeles, Lemmy penned a little ode to his adopted home, as if he was a teenager just starting out in the music business rather than 44 as he then was. Perhaps inescapably, Lemmy wrote a bouncy rock and roll riff, with plenty of room for barroom piano and saxophone as the song progresses, in a similar style to 'Black Leather Jacket' and in keeping with the broader musical brief and sheer authenticity that the band were pursuing. Unfortunately, even this mild drift into new territory would be largely curtailed from here on.

'Make My Day' (Burston/Campbell/Kilmister/Taylor)

Returning to their core mission statement, the band rip into a nasty riff and step up several gears to remind listeners that they are still capable of throwing in a raging rocker to appease their more traditional audience. Lyrically this is a quick take on one night stands and groupies and seems to consist of a series of chat up lines stitched together to form a lyric. The prospect of a longer-term relationship is constantly alluded to but, emphatically, not what is on offer.

As a song, this is just a smidge too 'identikit Motörhead' to really catch the imagination, but there are a lot of great tunes here besides.

'R.A.M.O.N.E.S.' (Burston/Campbell/Kilmister/Taylor)

Lemmy made little secret of his love for the American punk originators, mostly because he knew an amped-up amphetamine-fuelled rock and roll band when he heard them. Surprisingly credited to the whole band, this is a one-minute thirty-second punk thrash with shouted gang vocals and a great deal of affection for its subject. Lemmy betrays his inner nerd by listing every member of the Ramones, at that time, in his lyrics. The trio re-recorded the song in 2006, around the time of *Kiss Of Death*, but couldn't quite recapture the loosely shambolic love and irreverence that characterises this ridiculously enjoyable song. It was written specifically as a tribute to the band and Lemmy was delighted when the Ramones played it live, and they even recorded a studio version as a bonus track for their final album, *Adios Amigos!,* in 1995.

'Shut You Down' (Burston/Campbell/Kilmister/Taylor)

This is a startlingly heavy Motörhead rocker that almost sounds out of place amongst the other musical avenues being explored here. Referencing the form of a 'Dear John' letter, it is basically a lyric vituperatively talking about the end of a relationship. There are a couple of lines that could be read as a joke, though:

> Like to stay but you got too weird
> Don't look right since you grew that beard

Sometimes it is hard to tell when Lemmy is simply having a laugh or just coming up with the daftest rhymes he can think of.

'1916' (Kilmister)

The sound of an aged and cracked voice (presumably sung from his place in Heaven) relating an anti-war tale of a 16-year-old sent to the front line of the First World War is harrowing for many reasons. One of which is the bare vocal and the evident strain put on it. There are no humorous lines here and no sign of the rest of the band. The keyboards and drum machine are played by the producer underneath the aching cello that dominates the sound. Lemmy puts his knowledge of history to good use and produces another poetic lyric that enhances his reputation. If ever there was a doubt about his vehement anti-war stance, here's the stark proof.

Using the folk ballad form to stunning effect, this has all the traits of a traditional song, combined with a melancholy outlook, which would grace any folk club in the land. The only negatives are the vocals, as they can't quite reach the notes required and belie the stated age of the narrator. Nevertheless, this is a striking and uncharacteristic end to a Motörhead album that lingers in the memory.

Related recordings

'Dead Man's Hand' (Burston/Campbell/Kilmister/Taylor)

This scorching Cowboy gambling song recalls the band of a decade previous, but it was probably relegated to a b-side as it shares a similarity with the chorus melody of 'Ridin' With the Driver'. It is another signature Motörhead tune that might have been a contender to replace 'Make My Day' were it not for the chorus consideration.

There is a crazy opening riff that stays with the song all the way through, there are definitive battering drums from Philthy and it sounds like the band felt they were in competition with the heaviest bands of the era when they came up with this monster. The phased and fractured ending is a masterstroke and the song itself deserves re-evaluation and a far wider hearing.

'Eagle Rock' (Burston/Campbell/Kilmister/Taylor)

A no-nonsense rousing rock and roll song in an inimitable style, this has a great Philthy break, mad soloing from Phil and Wurzel, and a wonderful joy at its heart. They were obviously enjoying themselves immensely when this was recorded and it was unfairly banished to a b-side when it came out originally. Thankfully, it is much easier to find now.

March Or Die (WTG/Epic/Sony, August 1992)

Personnel:
Lemmy Kilmister: vocals, bass
Phil Campbell: guitars
Wurzel: guitars
Philthy Animal Taylor: drums
Tommy Aldridge: drums
Mikkey Dee: drums
Slash: guest guitar
Ozzy Osbourne: guest vocals
Produced at Music Grinder Studios, Los Angeles, 1991-1992 by Peter Solley and Billy Sherwood.
Highest chart place: UK: 60
Running time (approximate): 46:46

At the same time as *1916*'s success, Sharon Osbourne got in touch and asked if Lemmy would write a few sets of lyrics for Ozzy's next album, Ozzy commenting that he was okay at starting a lyric, but he was having trouble getting whole songs down. According to Lemmy, 'she made me an offer I couldn't refuse', and he worked extremely fast – Ozzy recounted that he wrote six sets of lyrics and read a book in four hours and 'the [lyrics] were all great'. Ozzy used four of the lyrics on his quadruple-platinum *No More Tears* album in 1991, and one of them also became a huge hit single in America for him, the tender and uncharacteristic ballad 'Mama, I'm Coming Home'. It finally put Lemmy on a financially stable footing for the rest of his life.

Lemmy was often heard to remark that: 'I made more money out of writing those four songs for Ozzy than I made out of fifteen years of Motörhead – ludicrous, isn't it!'

It was a surprisingly fertile time and, as usual, it would lead to darker times ahead because nothing ever ran smoothly for Motörhead.

During the recording phase of their next album, Philthy departed for the final time, his drumming in tatters. Making urgent use of his phone book, Lemmy called anyone who might be available to complete the recordings. Tommy Aldridge (ironically known for his stint with Ozzy Osbourne) was experienced and could step in at a moment's notice but hadn't been part of the writing process, which proved to be a barrier. The band were in a bind, though, and needed a drummer who was on the spot. Aldridge was seen as a safe pair of hands (and legs!) but not necessarily the choice the band would have made if it had not been an emergency.

'Stand' (Burston/Campbell/Kilmister)
Whether it was the loss of Philthy or just an opportune moment, this is the sound of Lemmy picking himself up and giving himself a pep talk. The music for this was by Phil and Wurzel using a stand-in drummer when it was initially

put together as a demo. Part of the reason for this was that Phil and Wurzel were in England while Lemmy was in Los Angeles.

When Tommy Aldridge was hastily roped in to cover for Philthy, he only really had the demos to work from and that's apparent here. He provides a standard rock beat, only deviating at the mid-chorus and for the underwhelming opening and closing sections.

Even at this early stage, it is clear that the band are floundering: there is a woolly thump to the drums that suggests the eye on the production ball was dropped, there's the feeling that everything is just a little behind the beat and the riffs are not as sharp or memorable as the previous album. Lemmy sounds almost bored singing this and he is the writer, which does not bode well for the rest of the songs.

'Cat Scratch Fever' (Ted Nugent)
Lemmy liked a good tune and, regardless of Ted's ultra-right-wing political stance, felt that the band should cover this 1977 nugget. The lyrics are sexist, even by the standards of the 1970s, and seem to suggest that every woman has the hots for the main character as he can please them every time. It makes some of Lemmy's words look positively liberal and politically correct by comparison.

The opening ancient blues-rock riff is tired and clumsy, but it's the pace that ruins it all. It's a strange thing to suggest that a Motörhead song should be faster, but that is precisely what's wrong here. The chorus is as bored sounding as 'Stand' and, believe it or not, this is actually slightly better as a cover than the original version.

'Bad Religion' (Burston/Campbell/Kilmister)
A typically scathing attack on organised religion and, particularly, TV evangelists, Lemmy goes all out to denounce the clergy and the Christian faith and uses Bible language to press his point home. The first chorus sums up his attitude:

Bad Religion, Bad Religion
I need no Gods or Devils, I need no Pagan rites
Bad Religion, Bad Religion
I need no burning crosses to illuminate my nights
HEY, HEY You hear me now, you hear me now
HEY, HEY For thou art Judas, the mark of Cain be on thy brow
Evangelistic Nazis, you cannot frighten me
The name you take in vain shall judge you for eternity

A spirited chugging guitar riff fades in as the opening but, once established, it is repeated for too long before the crunching and memorable main riff kicks in. Aside from the poor chorus melody, specifically around the title words, this is a song that would have fitted *1916* brilliantly and which astonishingly uses a brief sample (a first for Motörhead) of an evangelist exhorting his audience to give him money. The solos are beautifully melodic and the mid-paced crawl of the music gives the lyrics weight, while the straight rock drumming actually suits this anti-Christian cousin to 'Just 'Cos You Got The Power'. The vituperative vocals are a little blunted (probably in an attempt to disguise the message and produce a more commercial sound) and lower in the mix, but this is one of only two or three good songs on the album.

'Jack The Ripper' (Burston/Campbell/Kilmister)

Tommy produces an opening salvo on the drums to remind the listener that this is a Motörhead album, but the guitar riff sounds like a soft rock imitation of the band and the repetition is grating. Peter lathers on the production tricks in an effort to pull things out of the mire, but the key change into the middle eight (and the accompanying verse) is a step too far and the solos are formulaic. The use of the keyboards to back up the melody has none of the bravery of those on *1916* and this just seems to be another means to emulate the success of the previous album without possessing the equivalent number of great songs.

Throughout this album, the lyrics adopt a serious tone and show little of the wit or wordplay that Lemmy was capable of. Not necessarily an odd choice of subject matter, Jack the Ripper is a worldwide phenomenon, yet the lyrics are confused and contradictory at times. Referring to Spring-heeled Jack might look good on paper, but they are two extremely different stories: Spring-heeled Jack is an urban legend of early Victorian folklore (arguably, the first superhero as he appeared to dress up in a monstrous costume and to be able to make inhuman leaps) while Jack the Ripper was, infamously, the first serial killer to capture both the public's and the media's attention in the late Victorian era.

'I Ain't No Nice Guy' (Kilmister)

Lemmy was extremely happy with this song and talked about it with real pride. It is unfortunate that it is an underwhelming and mediocre ballad that attempted to accentuate the bad guy image but failed to really engage the listener, whether through a syrupy lyric or a leaden pace. Arguably the lyrics could be read as a realisation that the protagonist has come to a moment of clarity in their life and is looking back with regret at some of the choices they have made, but the overwhelming feeling the words portray is a little more cynical and self-knowing. As a commercially minded single, it had the obligatory guest appearances from Ozzy and Slash, but short circuits the expected heavy metal pedigree by fitting them into a folk paced duet of repentance. Some listeners will undoubtedly hear it as a reflective and honest portrayal of remorse, but the music lets it down. The acoustic guitar and piano introduction carry on for far too long, encompassing the first chorus, before giving up in favour of a power ballad middle eight, which features the obligatory soulful solo from Slash. By the time a (synthesized) string section enters the fray, the game is up. This is the only track Philthy appears on and, given the insipid and no-frills nature of his contribution here, it is no surprise that he was retired for the final time. Ozzy makes his contribution but doesn't appear to revel in the song. Still, he was returning a favour to a mate and he gives the duet his attention.

'Hellraiser' (Kilmister/Ozzy Osbourne/Zakk Wylde)
Given its multi-platinum lineage, this (arguable) cover should be an album highlight. However, it is plodding where it should be sprinting and it merely sounds like a space-filler, as if the band were lacking in songs and alighted on this recent collaboration. Ironically, it doesn't sound much better on Ozzy's *No More Tears* album. It's about as hellraising as a baby shower for Gwyneth Paltrow and everyone appears lifeless both playing and singing this dirge, with the exception of the guitar figure that punctuates the song throughout, undoubtedly from Phil. Lemmy tries to put some power behind his bass work, but it doesn't come across well. Maybe it's the commercially minded sheen from producer Billy Sherwood that kills the atmosphere, but that doesn't account for the rest of the album. This song was recorded at a session following the album's completion; hence the debut appearance of future mainstay Mikkey Dee on drums and it is a very anonymous beginning to his career in the band.

The lyric embellishes the joys of the rock and roll lifestyle, although it also implies that there is loneliness and regret attached to it. Repeating the first verse as the third verse shows a distinct lack of inspiration for the song.

When the song was then appropriated for use as the title music for *Hellraiser III: Hell On Earth* no one thought to revisit the words to give them a more integrated outlook for the movie. That kind of sloppiness is sometimes notable on this album and is partly why the album is such a disappointment.

'Asylum Choir' (Burston/Campbell/Kilmister)
This is a corking tune and probably the most interesting song on the album. The opening riff isn't promising, but the chorus lead guitar embellishments are sublime. Shaking off the somewhat torpid production and the rampant bid for commercialism, this single track hints at what might have been. It has a genuinely memorable chorus (which is impressive given the wordiness involved) and it has a creepy edge to the music that fits the central theme of madness and insanity. Again the solo is poor to start with, but it turns into something extraordinary and surprisingly inventive after the drums briefly jump out in the mix, although that suggests that the two parts of the solo were played by the two lead guitarists and then spliced together to achieve the desired effect. The drumming gives the whole song impetus, rather than hindering its progress, and there are the distinct glimmerings of a great song with a fine chorus poking through.

'Too Good To Be True' (Burston/Campbell/Kilmister)

A standard rock and roll number that Motörhead could write in their sleep appears to have accidentally been recorded when they *were* asleep. There is nothing here that couldn't have been done a whole lot better by any number of bands. Lyrically there seems to be an admission of romantic frailty, of regret for a departed love, and the chorus encapsulates that with the protagonist in contemplative mood:

Cold and lonely without you
Don't know if I can make it through
Maybe you'll hear this song
Been gone way too long
Too good to let it go, too good to be true

There is a finer song struggling to get out, but this is the cracked shell of the result.

'You Better Run' (Kilmister)

A blatant blues bass riff strolls through this unimaginative tune and the piano adds little, if anything, to this blunderbuss miss. Slash lends a hand on rhythm guitar, but it isn't noticeable. The drumming is a little too rock-oriented and the guitar solos are overly long and utterly pointless. Placing this in an acoustic setting and slowing the pace further could prove to be a smart rearrangement that might well have reinvigorated the song entirely.

Not afraid to have fun and mess around with their own songs (especially when offered a reasonable fee), this was re-recorded and became 'You Better Swim' for the 2004 *SpongeBob SquarePants* movie! Making a little more of an effort, the lyrics were overhauled to ensure this version was all the more unique.

'Name In Vain' (Burston/Campbell/Kilmister)

The weirdest thing about this song is that it's totally forgettable, even while it is being listened to. It has a neat little opening riff, which is dulled by the constant repetition, but it doesn't even shine amongst the dross that's here. This has a strange, almost country music break after the bland rock and roll of the rest of the music around it, but aside from that, the whole track falls flat on its formulaic face. The words sound like a petulant teenage boy wrote them about a girl that had the good sense to leave him, although the intent of the lyrics was undoubtedly different. Maybe these were discovered on the inside of a cigarette packet from 1964 and were used because nothing else came to mind.

'March Or Die' (Kilmister)

Endeavouring to emulate the vibrant anti-war message of '1916', and using a similarly funereal pace, this has a crushing martial beat and a synthesized (almost industrial) soundscape that attempts to mash together the claustrophobic terror of 'Orgasmatron' with a thudding indictment of warfare. The lyrics are fierce and angry at the waste of human lives and the writer acquits himself well. That the song doesn't entirely succeed is partly down to the uninspired production and partly down to the monotonous plod that takes the sharp edge from the song. If Al Jourgensen (of Ministry and Revolting Cocks fame) had been able to produce or remix this track, the result could have been electrifying.

This was a disappointing end to an album that had a lot riding on it and it was rewarded with their lowest chart placing ever, even lower than their debut.

Related recordings
'Hell On Earth' (Kilmister)
Recorded for the *Hellraiser III: Hell On Earth* soundtrack, along with the song 'Hellraiser' itself, this was part of a further session for the album but paid for by Victory Records (who were releasing the soundtrack) rather than their record label, hence the change of producer to Billy Sherwood. The lyrics, and attribution of a single songwriter, suggest that this song was written specifically for the movie rather than cannibalised from a previous song.

While the band were recording the final sessions for the album, the area surrounding the studio in South Central Los Angeles erupted into riots, arson and looting following the acquittal of four Police officers charged with excessively beating Rodney King. The incident was extremely public as the footage had been shown on prime time television and was deemed so newsworthy that it was repeated on news programmes around the world. Music Grinder studios were right in the path of the rioters and live footage was showing on the TV in the lounge of the studio. Perhaps apocryphally, Lemmy has been quoted as saying that he was recording the vocals for 'Hell On Earth' (or 'Hellraiser') when the riots were taking place.

Boasting a similarly oppressive sound world to the album's title track, this might well be Lemmy having a second crack at the same musical subject matter or simply looking for variations on a theme. Here, Mikkey's sophomore appearance for Motörhead is virtually indistinguishable from a drum machine and, along with the uncharacteristically slow 'Hellraiser', seems to be a particularly odd audition for the band. Nevertheless, they must have liked his style and personality because he spent the next twenty-three years behind his kit.

A rumbling bass is accompanied by Mikkey's martial thumping drums throughout the entire song and the only sign of Phil or Wurzel is in the two brief and strangled guitar solos that pop up to remind listeners of their existence. Instead of singing (and, yes, he does sing usually), Lemmy recites the grimly apocalyptic lyrics in a throaty gargle that builds on the poetry voice he deployed for 'Orgasmatron'. There is a recognisable chorus, albeit with a male backing vocalist (presumably not Wurzel!) to do the actual singing, which lends a further heaviness to the doom metal trappings the tune exhibits. It is a great shame that this song hasn't been added to reissues of *March Or Die,* as it would balance out some of the more disappointing numbers on show. As it is, 'Hell On Earth' is buried away on rare soundtracks or expensive box sets (*Stone Deaf Forever!*).

Bastards (ZYX, November 1993)

Personnel:
Lemmy Kilmister: vocals, bass
Phil Campbell: guitars
Wurzel: guitars
Mikkey Dee: drums
Produced at A&M and Prime Time Studios, Hollywood, August 1993 by Howard Benson.
Highest chart place: UK: Did Not Chart
Running time (approximate): 47:50

While Phil Carson had overseen the band throughout the *1916* period, during the recording of *March Or Die,* he had been headhunted to become Chairman of Victory Records (hence Motörhead's *Hellraiser III: Hell On Earth* soundtrack appearance) and he had reluctantly stepped down from his management work. At this point, the band's management became a little murky: a couple of sources claim that the band was being managed by an individual named Doug Banker (surely a pseudonym and, worryingly, rhyming slang which should have tipped the band off in short order) while other sources insist that Sharon Osbourne was offering her undoubted expertise to them. Whoever was involved, Motörhead were floundering and the contract they had signed with WTG/Epic/Sony was for individual albums rather than a guaranteed number. The contract was specifically written to ensure the label had an option for another album, but there was no firm commitment for one. Given the poor sales and reception of *March Or Die,* it was somewhat inevitable that the record company would allow the contract to lapse and would never request a third album.

The inexperienced but hugely enthusiastic Todd Singerman entered the frame at this time, pestering Lemmy that he should be managing the band and in charge of their career. In a period of calm, this offer might not have been taken up, but the band required solid management and a stable plan for their future as they had been battered by their sudden commercial and critical downfall. Lemmy took the bait and, finally, settled with management that he felt he could trust, and Todd would go on to manage the band until their dissolution, and beyond.

Todd arrived at a crucial time. He was listed as their manager on *March Or Die* but found himself with the unenviable task of finding a new record label that would support the band through another turbulent time. What he came up with was ZYX Records, a German dance music (!) label that 'offered us the most money.' Beggars cannot be choosers and, in their favour, the label was very enthusiastic about their new signing. The sticking point was that they had poor European distribution, no presence at all in the US and they had no idea how to market a heavy rock and roll band. Enthusiasm can only get you so far, so ZYX were the proud owners of *Bastards,* a blistering return to form that virtually nobody heard.

'On Your Feet Or On Your Knees' (Burston/Campbell/Mikkey Dee/Kilmister)

This is Mikkey's full-length debut and he is quite clearly out to impress. Complex rhythmic patterns and some sly time changes are at work on this battering revival of the heavy Motörhead sound. Gone are any attempts at commercialism and in its place comes a raging and authentic rock band clawing their way back to the top.

As if to signal a return to their roots, they open the album with the sound of a crackly vinyl record and then a sudden scratch jumps to the angry and serrated riff. Highly regarded punk and metal producer Howard Benson was contracted for the first of his four eventual productions and here he is already making his mark with a clean but heavy production that doesn't swamp the songs or resist those little touches of innovation that can be crucial to how an album turns out. The vinyl sample is one example.

The lyrics seem to be infected by the dourness and fear that reflected the global news of the Iraq War, the LA riots and the repercussions of the ongoing racism visible throughout the US. Lemmy was openly anti-racist (he could hardly have been anything else: his love of Little Richard and many others was incontrovertible) and the Rodney King fallout still seemed to inform his worldview. At the age of 47, he rediscovered his fury and sense of outrage.

'Burner' (Burston/Campbell/Dee/Kilmister)

Nowhere is this more evident than here. It is almost like Lemmy just continued adding more verses to the previous song and then created a new chorus. The opening lines make some very unsettling allusions:

Riots in the burning street
Crystal night outside
Brutal music in the night
Enough to make you cry

The writer is deliberately referencing the Nazi-inspired Kristallnacht ('Crystal Night', named after the shards of broken glass strewn over the streets) of October 1938 in Germany, where thousands of windows of Jewish-owned shops, homes and synagogues were smashed and Jews were attacked and intimidated. The protagonist of the song is protesting at the anti-Semitism that they see all around them and Lemmy sings 'I am the voice of broken glass', which has a double meaning: firstly, the writer is standing up for the rights of Jews, while secondly, he is noting that his own vocals are hardly sweet and tender.

The music accompanying this is suitably savage and unrelenting. The tune moves at a blistering pace and Mikkey puts some intricate polyrhythms into the chorus while both guitarists play like they have just auditioned for Metallica. Bruising and ferocious, this is the sound of a hardened Motörhead as never before.

'Death Or Glory' (Burston/Campbell/Dee/Kilmister)

The seriously vicious anti-war lyrics continue with what appears to be Lemmy's second attempt at 'March Or Die', this time nailing it with precision. Rather than go for the individual view of '1916' this sports a macro historic reading and takes the listener on a lengthy historical journey of conflicts and clashes throughout the ages; from Roman gladiators via Vikings and Spartans through to the First and Second World Wars (and a lot more in between) the lyrics read like the worst series of reincarnations ever visited upon a man:

> I was at Moscow, burning in my tank
> I was at Shiloh, marching in the ranks
> I was a Sturmbannführer fighting in Berlin
> I was a Russian hero, dying for Stalin

There are no jokes in this song, no double meanings. This is just a litany of death without any glory.

Surging along on Mikkey's pounding drums, upping the pace even further, this has all the hallmarks of speed metal and the musicianship to back it up. The middle eight pulls the music into a fascist march (Lemmy contributing 'hey!'s that miss 'heil' by a whisker of a vocal consonant) while the guitarists scratch and squeal atonally at their instruments just to ensure that no one misses the point. The return to the main riff is heralded by some brutal punishment of the drum kit and then everyone heads back into warp speed.

The final cry of 'Auf Stehen!!!' signals the end of the song with a deliberate full stop. In translation, this means 'stand up' and the way it is bellowed here suggests that the setting is a prison camp in Germany during World War II.

'I Am The Sword' (Burston/Campbell/Dee/Kilmister)

Changing lyrical tack somewhat, the Crusades are next on the list of targets for Lemmy's pen. Lamenting the use of religion as an excuse for murder, this time the protagonist is a soldier of God, and poring over their misguided belief that they are somehow righteous in their mission the words underline the steely determination of these warrior zealots, embodied in their talismanic swords.

A striking riff introduces proceedings and its limited use gives it a lustre that blanket repetition would have ruined. Reining back slightly on the speed this would still not qualify as mid-paced and the attack that every musician puts into this is thrilling to behold.

'Born To Raise Hell' (Kilmister)

Inevitably there is a return to the fun-loving side of the band, but after that quartet of seriousness, it can't come as a surprise. Another crack at the same subject matter as 'Hellraiser' produces a better result in every way while the single songwriter credit suggests that another commission has come through, especially as this song reappeared on the soundtrack to the film *Airheads*less than a year later. A feather-light tale of rock musicians trying to get their demos on the radio but accidentally taking the DJs hostage instead, the lyrical tone suits the comedy intent of the movie and the film features another cameo from the ubiquitous Lemmy. For the soundtrack album, the song was re-recorded with additional vocals from Ice-T (Body Count) and Whitfield Crane (Ugly Kid Joe) to enhance its chances when it was released as a single but, sadly, it is as poor as it sounds.

The basic rock and roll undertow is enhanced by the crisp drumming and the committed vocal, but it has an air of déjà vu about it in both music and lyrics. Part of its problem is that it has a prolonged running time (almost 5 minutes) that the song just can't support. It is an enjoyable boogie, but it has little to recommend it within Motörhead's back catalogue as a whole, although it outdoes 'Hellraiser' in every way.

'Don't Let Daddy Kiss Me' (Kilmister)

Another solo contribution, this wasn't writing for hire but a subject that Lemmy felt he had to address. It is a surprising issue to put into a slow ballad form and one that only partially succeeds. Paedophilia and child sexual abuse is hardly a topic for a rock song, generally, but it was a concern that Lemmy was able to articulate well. Laudable sentiments they may be but it is both hard to listen to (emotionally) and lacking a strong enough vocal. The lyrics are harrowing from beginning to end and the bleakness of the outlook is gut-wrenching. It's quite clear that Lemmy means to shock with these words, it's just the style of the tune that gets in the way of the message. Long gone are the days of 'Jailbait' and its don't ask/don't tell coyness.

Lemmy has frequently been quoted saying that 'they never look like us [rock and roll fans], they always look like them [suits, ties, smart clothes]' but the conviction of Ian Watkins, frontman and primary songwriter for Welsh nu-metal alt-rock band Lost Prophets in 2013 on multiple counts of child abuse, has sadly negated that view in a single disastrous example.

A frail and bare voice is only joined by piano and acoustic guitar for the early parts of the song, while the introduction of a mournful electric guitar figure is a herald for the battering power ballad middle eight, which doesn't suit the subject matter at all. The vocals are somewhat strained, partially with emotion and partially because the higher notes are hard to reach.

It is a strange place to put such a song as it kills the momentum of the album. Placing it first or last on the album may well have improved the running order in that regard. There is a longer than usual gap between this and the next song.

'Bad Woman' (Burston/Campbell/Dee/Kilmister)

Placing this formulaic ode to the titular bad woman straight after one of the most emotive and cutting lyrics of their entire career is, to say the least, ill-judged. The atmosphere is ruined by the rock and roll piano, bar room swing and tongue in cheek words of this perfectly acceptable album cut because of its awful position on the album. There is a different band at work here and one that needs to understand the dynamics and flow that a great album shows. That this is a great album is in spite of this cack-handed lack of attention to detail.

'Liar' (Burston/Campbell/Dee/Kilmister)

A brooding tune, which makes up with heaviness what it lacks in tempo, attempts to pull the album out of the slump it has got itself into. There is a chorus section placed in the music, but there is no recognisable hook to fill it (unless repeating 'Liar' or 'Killer' at the start of a verse can be interpreted as approximating a chorus). The drums are a little too sharp and bright at this point and could have been muted slightly to reflect the muddy feel that permeates the other instruments.

'Lost In The Ozone' (Burston/Campbell/Dee/Kilmister)

Pulling themselves back up with the tale of a stranded mariner (serving as a well-chosen metaphor for the loneliness everyone suffers when there is no God); this is the start of a rapid and welcome improvement that, thankfully, carries on to the end of the album. Rather than just a ballad, this comes in a heavy rock disguise (there is more than a hint of Guns 'N' Roses in the initial riff) and there is even space for a bass solo of sorts.

'I'm Your Man' (Burston/Campbell/Dee/Kilmister)

A rejuvenating and quirky riff brings everything back into order for the final stretch and it spends time rocking like the 1980s never ended. The lyrics finally regain their sense of humour. For example, how about the following:

> I can't move if I don't sing
> I can't stand, I got no chair

Or

> Can't see me, I'm the man, laid in bed
> Can't see me, give a damn, Motörhead

There is always a difficulty in sustaining both great tunes and fine lyrics over a whole album and Motörhead are no exception, but they really try hard here. And no, this is not a Wham! cover for anyone daft enough to ask...

'We Bring The Shake' (Burston/Campbell/Dee/Kilmister)

Fired up again, the band hit the ears with a chrome-plated riff and a renewed desire to bring rock back to the masses, complete with a catchy chorus and a spectacular tune. Back on form and nailing their sound for the next 20 years (kind of), Motörhead thrill with a biting lyric about rebellion (with a

93

sly glance towards fighting for your right to party) and a weirdly metallic monotone vocal.

Some interesting new guitar sounds are evident from the band and there is both a raucous solo and a sudden drop out that adds to the vocal impact. The song ends all too soon, a sure sign that it has legs, and the clichéd finales are all too evident by their absence.

'Devils' (Burston/Campbell/Dee/Kilmister)
This is monstrous psychedelic rock that could have been Hawkwind if it wasn't so brutally turbocharged. It all starts with a remarkable riff that builds and builds to the effervescent chorus, and then keeps on building until the song seems fit to burst. There may be a solo too many, but it doesn't detract from the sheer exuberance of the playing. It's almost as if a weight has been lifted from the band. Phil seems to be channelling a heavy metal Robert Fripp (King Crimson) while the band throw in a great slice of psych-rock that captures the joy of the lyrics and Lemmy's tuneful vocal additions. It may be called 'Devils', but the repeated refrain right to the end is 'angels in my heart tonight' and it sounds exultant.

Thus ends one of the finest comeback albums of the 1990s.

Related recordings
'Laugh At The Devil' (Clarke/Kilmister)
Fast Eddie Clarke. Recorded: January 1994. Found on: It Ain't Over Till It's Over (CD)

Eddie finally got around to making his debut solo album in 1994 (after Fastway had been put to bed) and the result was *It Ain't Over Till It's Over*. Burying any lingering rancour, Eddie invited Lemmy to contribute vocals and lyrics to a tune (although Eddie apparently forgot that Lemmy needed the guitars tuned half a step down so he could sing comfortably). The resulting almost-Motörhead reunion was rather hamstrung by Eddie's forgetfulness, the pedestrian drumming involved and the lack of Lemmy's bass. Lemmy gets into character and warns the listener not to laugh at the Devil as he will find you and punish you. The song stands as a bottom drawer Motörhead recording, where it could have been a highlight on side two of *Iron Fist*, which is ironic as it was also produced by Will Reid Dick. As a 'bonus' early Motörhead song, it has its charms, but it is also a bit of a missed opportunity.

The song was re-recorded for the debut album by Wurzel's new band Leader Of Down, *Cascade Into Chaos*, in 2008/9 and they rightly asked Eddie to play the guitars on the track. Lemmy then re-recorded his vocals in 2010 to complete the song for future release. Leader Of Down's debut was posthumously released in 2018 and the album re-recording has a different, more complicated arrangement and a much heavier slant than the original, sonically in the same area as Motörhead's recordings with Cameron Webb.

The song holds up better here and the vocals sound less strained than the 1994 take due to the rearrangement, but the drumming is overly busy at times and Lemmy still misses out on playing the bass part. The comparison between the two versions is fascinating.

Sacrifice (Steamhammer/SPV/CBH, March 1995)

Personnel:
Lemmy Kilmister: vocals, bass
Phil Campbell: guitars
Wurzel: guitars
Mikkey Dee: drums
Produced at Cherokee Studios, Hollywood, November-December 1994 by Howard Benson, Ryan Dorn and Motörhead.
Highest chart place: Did Not Chartin the UK
Running time (approximate): 36:44

Back in 1994, the band felt they had been carrying Wurzel for a year or two. They recognised that his heart wasn't in the music as it had once been, and perhaps this was his response to the continuing troubled times for the band.

They had to accept his implied resignation when he left the *Sacrifice* sessions after his parts were completed. Some foreign releases went so far as to use a three-man photo of the band and to cut Wurzel from the credits entirely. The European issue wasn't so mean. Lemmy may have understood the quiet way Wurzel just retreated from the band, and the music business in general but grieved over the loss of another friend.

After the distribution debacle of *Bastards,* Todd searched for a more reliable label and ended up with CBH Records who were part of the huge German independent company SPV. Released under the label's heavy metal imprint Steamhammer, Motörhead had finally found a record company they could work with, and they did so for the next fifteen years.

The post-album admission that most of the words were 'nonsense' is indicative of the production line mentality of the time. Howard was, like producers past, distracted by his new and lucrative A&R job and spared little attention for the task at hand. That, combined with Wurzel's dissatisfaction, Lemmy's brief illness and his subsequent dismissive attitude to his lyric writing, led to a far poorer album than the world had been expecting.

'Sacrifice' (Burston/Campbell/Dee/Kilmister)
The opening drum salvo from Mikkey became a signature entrance to almost every album that followed, but here it still sounds fresh and exciting. He shows both his power and precision on this otherwise very two-dimensional standard rock song that only really comes alive when the chorus barges in. There's a thundering presence to the track and some spectacular drumming evident, but the actual tune seems to have got lost in the maelstrom. It is a stirring and guttural chorus, however, although quite what the lyrics are about is wide open to interpretation. The band loved the song enough to make it a regular part of their live set for years to come.

'Sex & Death' (Burston/Campbell/Dee/Kilmister)
The two big subjects that run throughout Motörhead's career are summed up in a single song. The bulk of the word count is given over to death (boys on the front line of World War I dreaming of the girl back home), while the sex part has very little devoted to it, being reduced to empty fantasy.

The riff recalls a couple of the poorer efforts on *Rock 'N' Roll* and thrashes about seemingly interminably (although this is the shortest song here), but at least it has a brief time to disappoint. The best part is the sudden dropout at the end. It was written, several sources agree, on the last day of recording and, sadly, it sounds like a last-minute throwaway to bring the album up to a reasonable time.

'Over Your Shoulder' (Burston/Campbell/Dee/Kilmister)
In contrast to the last song, someone was obviously delighted to have come up with this staggering riff, the grinding guitars roll along with force and purpose. There is a doom metal vibe to this that hits a musical g-spot even if the words are a bit jumbled. On this occasion, the lyrics must bow to the music, which will conjure up images of rows of headbangers nodding in unison to the all-conquering pulse of the riff. Lemmy called it 'a great favourite of mine', and that was entirely down to the riff.

'War For War' (Burston/Campbell/Dee/Kilmister)
No prizes for guessing what the subject matter concerns. Nicely fading in on a grinding riff that savagely continues throughout, the music echoes the feeling of a war machine chewing up soldiers, but the guitar solo is a real letdown as it works against the tenor of the track by being too straight and far from brutal. The danger of recording the vocals last shows itself here. If Phil had known what the song was about, he could have provided a completely new, and complementary, solo instead.

'Order/Fade To Black' (Burston/Campbell/Dee/Kilmister)
Lyrically this seems to be two sets of words welded together like scrap metal. Poetic in presentation, it is broken up into five stanzas. The odd-numbered stanzas look like this (and could be classed as a 'chorus' if mentioning the title is the criteria):

(Yes) bad blood, (yes) black night, (My God, yes) all the world
(Yes) red mouth (yes) insane, (yes, My God) Order
(See) firestorm (see) black death, (do you see) burning there
(Yes) red smile, (yes) white noise, fade to black, nobody cares

While, for the even-numbered verses, they read like staccato streams-of-consciousness:

Wake up now, try to run, howling pain, burn like sun, creep
and crawl, hiding place, out of breath, turn your face.

97

Evil grins, at the sight, tendon snap, red tonight,
Black inside, cancer grown, in your skin, in your bone.

Musically this is practically grindcore for the odd-numbered stanzas and then
there is a crunching gear change into an almost thrash metal tempo for the
even verses. This is a radical switch in both compositional and writing styles
for the band and it shows that they are still willing to experiment and innovate.
Calling it a song in the accepted sense is quite difficult as this has definite
progressive metal tendencies at its heart, although Phil still manages to squeeze
in a solo, this time in keeping with the music surrounding it.

The whole piece is a superb demonstration of Mikkey's drumming prowess,
regardless of the success (or otherwise) of the song, and reinforces Lemmy's
belief that Mikkey was the greatest drummer the band ever had.

'Dog Face Boy' (Burston/Campbell/Dee/Kilmister)

Phil and Wurzel both thought they were the inspiration for the title character,
as the lyrics allude to the touring rock band lifestyle and the effect it has on an
individual. The words try to camouflage the intent by talking about werewolves
and hinting at the American tradition of freak shows, but it fooled no one. It
is a song about feeling utterly wrecked and it has some fun with the lyrics.
Lemmy later revealed that he thought the words were about Phil, but only once
he had written them.

A standard Motörhead album track, this sinks into the mire of also-rans that
pepper many of their albums. There is nothing particularly wrong with it; it
just doesn't have the spark of inspiration that would have lifted it from the
third division. As the song comes to an end, Lemmy starts to sing with real
gusto and makes a couple of interesting vocal variations. If he had given the
whole song something similar, it might have turned out differently. This is one
of only two songs here that have a solo from Wurzel and he makes a good job
of it. The tail end of it is particularly noteworthy.

'All Gone To Hell' (Burston/Campbell/Dee/Kilmister)

With a riff plucked straight from *Orgasmatron* and a somewhat more
committed vocal, this has the makings of a fine addition to the back catalogue,
but the rather limp momentum, the poor use of the riff and the lack of a real
hook leave this song struggling to remain afloat. Laying bare the vocals at the
end of the song also highlights the poor state of Lemmy's voice when it was
recorded. If his singing is illustrating the song title, then it is very well done
because his voice is shot to pieces.

Phil pulls out an excellent solo to prove he can do it sometimes, but the end
result is that Phil is trying to put polish on a turd.

'Make 'Em Blind' (Kilmister)

This is a rare solo writing credit that bucks the lyrical trend by echoing the
dystopian science fiction nightmares of Hawkwind, predicting a bloody Earth

rebellion followed by a plague that the rebel humans then spread out into the universe. The plague, it is suggested, could be the people themselves:

Ten thousand worlds await us
But we shall only wreck them
Ten thousand times ten thousand
But we will still infect them

This is an entirely unique subject for a Motörhead song and one that could have travelled in the opposite direction and been covered by Hawkwind. What possessed Lemmy to come up with these lyrics is open for debate as he never wrote on a similar topic anywhere else in his writing. Clearly, something apocalyptic was on his mind. There are reputed to be three full sets of lyrics to this song and one wonders what the other two were like.

As for the backing, this is a sinuously rhythmic percussion-led tune with a ripe bass and a solo from Phil that twists and whines and screeches at various points. Wurzel seems conspicuous by his absence here.

Continuing to explore the boundaries of their self-imposed limits, this is another interesting demonstration of their collective desire to broaden their outlook and explore new avenues.

'Don't Waste Your Time' (Kilmister)
This second solo credit bolsters the first but is dissimilar in virtually every way: it features saxophone and piano, it changes lyrical direction abruptly from the earlier track and it is in stark musical contrast to its predecessor. The subtext implies that Lemmy is showing the world the variety of what he has to offer as a songwriter.

A sneakily positive lyric about living your life to the full is disguised by the fatalistic first verse:

Bet you're scared of dying, scared of death
Think you might choke on your final breath
Wanna go to Heaven, scared of Hell
Scared of the Devil and his tail as well

There is also a pointed line that brings up the spectre of heroin and its terrible consequences, which adds a dose of seriousness to an otherwise positive message.

Given the writer, it will not be a shock to learn that this is a jaunty and breezy rock and roll song to lift the spirits and raise the fun quotient.

'In Another Time' (Burston/Campbell/Dee/Kilmister)
A nihilistic philosophy permeates this melancholy reminiscence. There is a presentiment of doom here, not necessarily about Wurzel's imminent departure but a dawning realisation of mortality.

Influenced by Jake E Lee's contributions to Ozzy's recorded output, the initial riff could be from any of Ozzy's 1990s albums, but the chorus riff is all Motörhead and the solo is serpentine and bolstered with effects pedals to give it that suitably twisting sound. Significantly lacking in humour, there is, nevertheless, a rather fine song evident. Interestingly this was the song that was most altered from its initial writing session being almost unrecognisable when the recording was finished. Redeploying the vocal mannerism from 'We Bring The Shake' is a nice touch and the only drawback is the reappearance of the live ending that the band were so enamoured of in years past.

'Out Of The Sun' (Burston/Campbell/Dee/Kilmister)

In an unconscious nod to their previous album, the final song is another epic and somewhat psychedelic departure, written while Lemmy wasn't looking (okay, he was unwell) and consequently rather hard to fit the words into. The arrangement was a hurdle too, as there was room for two and a half verses but only a single chorus section. This odd structure was further complicated when Lemmy and his guitar roadie, Jaime Germaine, added more musical parts without informing the band.

This less than stellar effort featured the final solo from Wurzel and, by all accounts, it took an extremely long time to get it down (around 6 hours, according to Phil) which is perhaps why it is so pedestrian; Wurzel had given up by this point.

The lyrics talk about living on a cold planet, a frozen wasteland where 'trees are stone' and 'leaves [are] razor steel'. The images conjured are striking and the feel of the music and words act in harmony together. Lemmy was fully aware of the planetary crisis on the horizon, although he subverts expectations by singing of global cooling. It is a rare occasion when the title 'eco-warrior' can be placed upon him, but there it is.

Overnight Sensation (Steamhammer/SPV/CBH, October 1996)

Personnel:
Lemmy Kilmister: vocals, bass, harmonica, acoustic guitar
Phil Campbell: guitars
Mikkey Dee: drums
Produced at Ocean and Track House Recording Studios, Los Angeles, June-July 1996 by Howard Benson and Duane Baron.
Highest chart place: UK: Did Not Chart
Running time (approximate): 41:19

Reverting to the trio format (allegedly, Lemmy asked Phil if he could cover all the guitars and Phil said yes and that was it!), the band started work on yet another make-or-break album.

Genuinely the most disturbing thing about the new album was the cover photo: Mikkey is unrecognisable (the person in the picture looks about 14 years old and where did his blond hair go?!) and Lemmy had *shaved* his moustache off, which was both unsettling and previously unthinkable. That facial growth, along with his prominent mole, were undoubted trademarks for Lemmy and he had whimsically lost the moustache, perhaps to indicate another new beginning.

'Civil War' (Magnus 'Ax' Axelsson/Campbell/Todd Campbell/Dee)

With hindsight, Mikkey acknowledged that the loss of Wurzel changed the songwriting dynamic within the band. Wurzel was often responsible for the hard and dirty riffs and was less concerned with the more intricate musical perfectionism that Mikkey and Phil sometimes came up with. Perhaps unconsciously, this might be why Ax (guitarist for the band Swedish Erotica) gets a songwriting credit as he contributed to the initial sessions with Mikkey in Sweden. The musicians were looking for a harder tone in their riffs and Ax fitted the bill perfectly. There is also a rare credit for a second outside writer, Todd Campbell (son of Phil). There is a query about who actually penned the lyrics for this song, but the general consensus is that Todd was responsible because Lemmy doesn't get a credit at all.

Mikkey puts down a machine gun fast snare drum opening and then the whole band join in with a great buzzing riff and piledriver speed. The words could have been written by their usual lyricist and the tune itself is as impressive as they have ever produced. It is a very strong beginning to the album and a confident sign that the loss of Wurzel would not prove a fatal hindrance.

'Crazy Like A Fox' (Campbell/Dee/Kilmister)

Frank Zappa once asked 'does humour belong in music' and Lemmy would often reply 'yes!' There are several lyrical couplets where it is clear that he is just having fun with words: 'You must be an earthquake, Cause I'm shaking in my shoes' and 'You must be a guitar player, The way you're stringing me along'.

There is even a sweet nod to Ian Dury and the Blockheads when the line 'Oh mama, hit me with your rhythm stick' appears.

Musically this has a rock and roll heartbeat but smothered in heavy metal guitar and boasting a pounding gallop that brings to mind fox hunting in its literal sense and as an inevitable play on words. Despite its musical credentials, it has a firmly tongue-in-cheek lyric that raises the whole song to a new level. The bluesy harmonica from Lemmy is a beautiful touch.

'I Don't Believe A Word' (Campbell/Dee/Kilmister)
Starting with a blues-metal bass chug, this quickly establishes itself as a slow-paced highlight. Roughing up the semi-ballad form, this relies on blues repetition for its core interest and a laid-back approach for its timing. This is the way these songs should be done. Admittedly, the length of the song could have been cut down, but the basic undercarriage of the tune is sound. It was undoubtedly initially inspired by Lemmy's throbbing bass pulse, which emerged in rehearsals. In a rare break with tradition, this is sung in clean tones (without the double-tracking of the voice or the throat-wrenching growl that usually figures) and it gives the song greater weight and impact for its relative vocal fragility, especially when Lemmy sings against himself in the pre-chorus.

The words seem to have flowed as both the verses and choruses are packed with meaning. There is an aching melancholy, coupled with a bitter undertow, to the lyrics that suggest the writer had discovered a monumental betrayal in a close confidant.

'Eat The Gun' (Campbell/Dee/Kilmister)
A rather more identikit riff is bolted to a speeding rock beat and it gives the illusion of being an anti-war song before the essential double meaning is revealed. Whether he was feeling particularly lazy that day or he just couldn't focus, the lyrics consist of a series of short statements that are repeated several times. There is about as much subtlety to the song as Jethro Tull's 'Kissing Willie' and it has about as much staying power. The solos are strangled and a little ridiculous and that reflects the subject matter.

The 'Oh wow's that finish the song seem rather more feminine in tone and timbre, which either means that someone was roped in to provide these vocals or that Phil has been at the helium again...

'Overnight Sensation' (Campbell/Dee/Kilmister)
The dirty rumble of the bass echoes 'Orgasmatron,' but it quickly skips into a mid-tempo rocker that takes a light-hearted look at the career disasters that could befall any long-lived band. That is the voice of experience talking. If you detect any hints of irony in the lyrics, then you are definitely in the right area. A tidy riff supports a nice melody and the title track rises to the occasion.

The submerged wah-wah solo that is heard in the final stretch is also rather endearing. What is also evident is that the solos from Phil are less frequent and more subdued than previous outings, but maybe he is thinking about how to reproduce these songs live as a trio.

'Love Can't Buy You Money' (Campbell/Dee/Kilmister)

A blunt descending heavy metal riff is matched by the rasping sandpaper vocal that is smeared over this song. A bass solo is evident in the middle eight, which is unusual, and the choppy melody is surprisingly memorable. The tune is short, but that just gives it impact.

The words seem to be three random verses stitched together rather than having an overall aim or theme. The one thing the stanzas do have is a great feel for the rhythm being explored. While they may read as nonsensical or at least lacking in a subject, they do fit the music perfectly.

'Broken' (Campbell/Dee/Kilmister)

Unfortunately, the tired riff that begins proceedings is then further weakened by the over-used guitar figure that sits at the end of the riff. The chorus lacks a killer hook and the part where Lemmy's voice is put through a megaphone is best forgotten. The lyrics feel recycled and the momentum of the album suddenly seems to dip, as is often the case when two-thirds of the album has passed. What used to be the middle of the vinyl side two was usually the dumping ground for the songs that never quite achieved their potential (look at *Bastards* for another example). In this case, there is nothing dreadful about the song; it just occupies the space reserved for the also-rans.

'Them Not Me' (Campbell/Dee/Kilmister)

A blazing serrated riff is joined by a charging rhythm section and a razor blade vocal that streaks off almost before anyone has time to blink. The punk-influenced music suggests that this would suit a horror film soundtrack (*28 Days Later* immediately springs to mind), while the lyrics have a zombie movie edge to them. It might all be over in less than three minutes, but it has a vitality about it that cannot be denied.

There is an intricacy to the music, and a level of playing ability, that belies the perception of Motörhead as a simple rock band churning out the same material decade after decade.

'Murder Show' (Campbell/Dee/Kilmister)

A biting commentary on the human condition and the lowest common denominator media attention that results, there is an appalled heart beating at the centre of this song. Grittily listing the worst excesses of humanity, and their apparent desire to witness these atrocities, the onus is put on the voyeuristic viewer of these terrible crimes.

Attaching this to a rather too bright rock and roll riff is a mistake. There is room for piano accompaniment in several instances, even though it is not used, and the song suffers from the essentially jaunty nature of the music, which hugely undercuts the gravity of the lyrics.

'Shake The World' (Campbell/Dee/Kilmister)
Everyone starts at the same time on this pummelling tune. Somewhere underneath is a blues-rock base but the punk execution and rampant drumming disguise everything. It certainly shakes your speakers, even at low volumes. The words are distinctly pessimistic and the spoken word end line of 'nothing can go wrong' is echoed to the fade, in chilling manner.

There are a couple of buzzsaw riffs amidst this drum frenzy, and there is the odd calmer moment, but this is undoubtedly one of the heaviest songs here.

'Listen To Your Heart' (Kilmister)
Ending a fascinatingly impressive album on an acoustic concoction is a brave and surprising decision. There is a rock and roll groove at work here and the tempo is fast enough for true fans, but the acoustic guitars are a radical departure and, apart from a briefly audible electric solo, are present throughout. No one is going to mistake this for folk music, but the general tone is upbeat and the lyrics are in keeping with that. There is no humour or irony here, just a straight desire to communicate a positive message, and all attached to a naively hummable chorus. It's a fine ending to a confident-sounding trio debut.

Related recordings
'B4' (Nina C. Alice/Kilmister/Jim Voxx)
Skew Siskin. Recorded: March 1996 . Found on: Voices From The War or Devils Disciple (CD)
Skew Siskin supported Motörhead on several tours and, when there was a little downtime for Lemmy, he would often go into their studio in Germany and contribute to their songs. Usually, this would involve co-writing lyrics, but he did provide vocals and bass on rare occasions. Here he sings and adds his instrumental skill to an excellent song, worthy of both his name and talent. Skew Siskin take the sheer brutality of punk and combine it with the weight and musicianship of heavy metal. Nina C Alice's vocals have the power of Janis Joplin twinned with the punk attitude of Wendy O Williams, all set against the dizzyingly breakneck music, although they are an acquired taste.

This song encapsulates that perfectly and benefits from Lemmy's collaboration. It opens with a brilliantly mangled 'Ace of Spades' riff and it explodes into life quickly, the singers alternately duetting and taking single lines or verses for themselves. The heavy crunch of the track doesn't quite maintain the interest for the close to five minutes of its running time, but it comes awfully close.

'Tie Your Mother Down' (Brian May)
Lemmy. Recorded: 1997. Found on: Lemmy: Damage Case (CD)
Vocally, this is a surprisingly vigorous cover that Lemmy handles really well. Quite clearly, he doesn't have the range of Freddie Mercury, but he produces a very creditable performance. This is the first of the real cover versions that he lent his voice to, but nowhere near the last. In keeping with the majority of these contributions, Lemmy has no input on the musical side, but his singing is always distinctive.

Featuring a sturdy line-up (Ted Nugent on guitar, Rudy Sarzo on bass, old mate Tommy Aldridge on drums and future producer Bob Kulick on rhythm guitar) there's little to complain about on the musicianship front, although there is a decidedly heavy metal slant to proceedings, which means that this is a pretty impressive take on a song that might have been thought uncoverable. This paved the way for future tribute album contributions and was produced by old associate Billy Sherwood.

'It's A Long Way To The Top' (Bon Scott/Angus Young/Malcolm Young)
Lemmy. Recorded: 1997. Found on: Cover Me in '80s Metal (CD)
Not a surprising choice of cover, but the treatment of this tune is startling: there are drum machines, synth bass (!), and what appears to be a guitar synthesizer at work. Ozzy alumnus Jake E Lee is actually playing some of the guitars, but it's hard to tell from much of the music presented here. This instrumental mish-mash does not suit AC/DC at all. Lemmy does a fantastic job with the singing and the guitar work, such as there is, is committed and nicely played, but the electronic rhythm section and the weird synth swoops that pop up throughout are a shock on first listening. Indeed, they are a shock on every listen.

For some reason, this was then remixed by Wayne Hussey (The Mission UK), seemingly on an off day, at the request of the record company. This particular version has been re-released several times.

Snake Bite Love (Steamhammer/SPV/CBH, March 1998)

Personnel:
Lemmy Kilmister: vocals, bass
Phil Campbell: guitars
Mikkey Dee: drums
Produced at The Valley Studio, Los Angeles, January 1998 by Howard Benson and
Motörhead.
Highest chart place: UK: Did Not Chart
Running time (approximate): 44:53

Overnight Sensation was an unexpected success and the reason for that was
laid squarely at the significantly improved distribution by SPV. Motörhead, of
course, carried on their usual busy touring schedule until the rumblings for a
new recording were heard. Lemmy was off ill for a fortnight during the writing,
rehearsing and arranging stages of the new songs and came back to find that the
non-singers in the band had created a few issues around how he was going to
add lyrics and sing these strangely arranged songs. This is the reason *Snake Bite
Love* sounded a little different when it was unleashed upon the world. It was
also the reason why they had no backup songs that could be recorded. They
turned up with eleven tunes in various states of completion and that was it.

To be brutally honest, the best thing about this album is the rear booklet
photo: the band are all pictured laughing uproariously at something off-
camera.

'Love For Sale' (Campbell/Dee/Kilmister)
Phil chucks out another of his assured riffs, although this time more in the
style of AC/DC, but the body of the song is overly repetitive and the best part
of the track is the catchy chorus and that oft-repeated guitar part. Musically
this stands up pretty well and gets a fine bounce going before the verses stifle
the energy of the song. That little chorus melody is a memorable earworm,
however. The ghost of rockabilly is visible in the underlying rhythm.

There are no surprises in the lyrics, which concern strip clubs and pole-
dancing but not outright prostitution, although there is a hint of the light-
hearted about them. Given the speed of the rehearsals and the abbreviated
recording conditions, this song is a welcome opener that augurs well for the
music to come.

'Dogs Of War' (Campbell/Dee/Kilmister)
The grinding riff and the bludgeoning drumming cannot disguise the stuttering
arrangement that leads to Lemmy almost tripping over his own tongue,
attempting to jam words into the spaces that they have left for him. The lyrics
are, inevitably, a bit of a jumble, but it is the staccato singing that really brings
the song down. It might well have been better to leave it as an instrumental,

but that is not the band's way. Layering on an array of guitar sounds to disguise the paucity of what is on offer here is a feeble attempt that fails before it starts.

The words, and the form they take, are a continuation of the style first expressed on *Sacrifice*'s 'Order/Fade To Black' and they are about as successful. The unfortunate unconscious reference to the abysmal 'Dogs' from a decade previous doesn't inspire confidence either. The studio environment of the song is highly visible as it is clear that the singer would be unable to repeat this song in the live arena. In Motörhead terms, this makes the song virtually space-filler as playing their music to an appreciative audience was the major defining feature of the band.

'Snake Bite Love' (Campbell/Dee/Kilmister)
A cut and shunt tune that was initially recorded with one set of chords over the drum backing track and then returned to Mikkey's local studio in Sweden when Phil added a completely new set of riffs and chords because he disliked the first version so much. All this chopping and changing, on top of the pressure of time, inevitably led to a mish-mash title track that has no idea where it is going and little clue as to its ultimate destination.

Telling the listener that he wants to see a boa constrictor wrap itself around a victim is a pretty penetrable metaphor which he hammers home with a great deal of relish. His continued use of the zoo animal's motif is amusing the first time, but the idea palls after repetition.

You can certainly hear the strain put on the song by the constant shifting of the bedrock, but there is an interesting riff poking out underneath and a broad suggestion of rock and roll in the chassis. Just to bemuse the listener, there are a few sudden synthesizer flutters, which recall the classic opening tones to Hawkwind's 'Silver Machine' as a lead up to the squealing and unfettered solo.

'Assassin' (Campbell/Dee/Kilmister)
Against the throbbing rhythm section backdrop, Lemmy deploys his gargled spoken word vocal for this chunkily heavy clatter. There is a complex and intricate arrangement at work here and Mikkey drops in a time-changing percussive solo as a middle-eight which is fascinating as a songwriting variation but lacks the immediacy and melody of their better songs.

The lyrics are welded into the shape of the tune or just splattered wildly over the top, which again highlights the ill-prepared nature of the band at these sessions. The seemingly endless repetition of the title long outstays its welcome and the idea that assassins are a bad thing is beyond hackneyed.

'Take The Blame' (Campbell/Dee/Kilmister)
A blurred riff announces one of the fastest songs Motörhead ever recorded. Mikkey demonstrates his remarkable prowess and anchors this bludgeoning tune with aplomb. It's almost as if the band all took speed at the same time and just roared through this backing track before they remembered they were going to have to put words to it.

Everything slows down for the mid-section, where the sound of a Hammond organ can distinctly be heard, adding melody, and a surprisingly extravagant solo, to the brutal proceedings, although the player is unfairly left uncredited. The identity of the mystery keyboard player is most likely to be Mari Germaine, a long-term associate of the band.

The lyrics viciously and with scalpel-like efficiency target venal and selfish politicians the world over and no one is spared the vitriol of Lemmy's tongue.

'Dead and Gone' (Campbell/Dee/Kilmister)

Finding themselves running out of tunes altogether, Lemmy dredged up an ancient Sam Gopal tune he had written, 'The Sky Is Burning' (1969), and this surprisingly musically faithful rendition was the result. The melody and the essentially quiet nature of the song are kept intact (the psychedelic tabla trappings of the original are, however, a far distant memory), although there is time for a couple of brief full-band outbursts on the chorus (which presumably warranted the writing credits for Mikkey and Phil).

The lyrics were entirely rewritten for the occasion, although they aren't much darker than the original words, even though the themes are opened out into a more universal message. This is a very successful reinterpretation of an old song and it helps the album to overcome some of its many inadequacies.

'Night Side' (Campbell/Dee/Kilmister)

Declared by the entire band as the worst song they ever did, this has few redeeming features. Mikkey hates it and with good reason. One wonders why they didn't just leave it off, but the band just shrug and say, 'we had nothing else.'

A beautifully smeared guitar greets the listener, but it all collapses with the poor chorus, the clock-watching drumming and the uncharacteristic vocal, which sounds like Lemmy has terrible catarrh rather than giving us his usual guttural roar. It is evident that the lyrics were thrown together at the last minute (not unusual for Lemmy), but any inspiration was lacking in this clichéd and lacklustre tale of werewolves on the prowl.

The real giveaway that the band wanted to get this tune over with as soon as possible is that they employ a similar technique to the one Hawkwind used on 'Silver Machine (Requiem)' in 1979; the music is abruptly cut off to be replaced by the second division sound effect of an explosive damp squib followed by its windy aftermath...

The borderline silly guitar solo and the muscular middle eight are the only redeeming features of this underneath the barrel-scraping.

'Don't Lie To Me' (Kilmister)

Often a single songwriter credit would mean a slow song from the main man but not here. This is a rock and roll song dirtied up and given a metal makeover (especially with Phil's solo) which has a great deal in common with the heavy Elvis cover of 'Blue Suede Shoes' from 1990. Clearly calling out for piano accompaniment, the arrangement even makes sonic space for the contribution; it is an obvious oversight that no keyboard parts were recorded. If a comparison is needed, this appears to be 'Angel City' part two but without the brio or catchiness of the original.

Apparently, Lemmy doesn't want people to lie to him. That's the main thrust of the lyrical outpouring here, but it is monumentally ill-served by the relaxed good-time music on display.

'Joy Of Labour' (Campbell/Dee/Kilmister)
For once on this album, the lyrics and music work together to create a song that reflects the subject matter. A quick glance at the words shows that it is not a song about pregnancy but a very disturbing look at the Nazi concentration camps from the point of view of an SS guard. It is almost as if the writer watched *Schindler's List* but focused on one of the camp guards for their inspiration. There are no jokes in this one.

Often above the gates, but always prominently placed, all the concentration camps displayed the German phrase Arbeit Macht Frei. The most widely used translation of the motto means: work sets you free. Twisted around that becomes the 'Joy of Labour', a fatuous yet chilling reminder of the depths of evil the human race can sink to. Around the time of this album being written, there was a clear rise in anti-Semitism and a noticeable increase in neo-Nazi and fascist organisations, undoubtedly influencing the lyricist.

Musically this is accompanied by a grinding riff that is left bare of effects but finds itself attached to an almost goose-stepping rhythm track. Singing in a gravelly monotone for the verses, which adds real impact to the words, the chorus is sung in a higher register and this time, they remember to double track the vocals to produce a more pleasing vocal sound.

The only jarring note is sounded by the overly melodic solo that fades the song out, a miscalculation that seems to sum up this entire album.

'Desperate For You' (Campbell/Dee/Kilmister)
The band later admitted that there were two turkeys on this album and public opinion has identified this as the second clunker to be recorded for this benighted collection. The band tears off into another rockabilly tinged punk flight to nowhere. All bluster and intent and no real tune, this is a poor way to start rounding off an album, even if the punk influence brings a welcome looseness to an otherwise perplexing set of songs. There appears to be the phantom of a honky-tonk piano part in the mix, but the aim seems to be to finish the album as quickly as possible without thought for the mixing that needed to be done to complete the album. It all ends with the clichéd 'live' finale, which had been mercifully absent for some years. It illustrates how flawed the song is because the band can think of no better end to the track.

The deadline-concocted lyrics have a scattershot approach to them, much in the way that a blunderbuss might, and they have little to recommend them.

'Better Off Dead' (Campbell/Dee/Kilmister)

After 40 minutes of largely bewildering ear-blistering, the last song hoves into view. A patented blunt riff kicks off a decent little blur of a song. Mikkey is on top form here and Phil isn't far behind, both giving a creditable mugging-of-Metallica vibe while Lemmy puts a great deal of energy into both his playing and singing. Short, catchy and fun, it's only a pity that the rest of the album didn't have either the verve or the completeness of this tune. The swift and entirely appropriate ending doesn't wipe away the memory of this poor album, but it does leave the listener feeling that there was something good amidst the dross.

Related recordings

'Eve Of Destruction' (Barry McGuire)

Mike Batt and the Royal Philharmonic Orchestra. Recorded: 1998. Found on: Philharmania: All Time Great Rock Hits (CD)

This is a voice-stretching cover of a very old chart-topping song from 1965, but it works. Q: What do you get if you add Lemmy and female backing singers to an orchestral backing? A: Weird brilliance. Lemmy was asked to contribute to a Royal Philharmonic Orchestra album masterminded by maverick producer and arranger Mike Batt, an acquaintance of Lemmy's who he first met in 1967. The songs would be covers of broadly rock songs ('A Whiter Shade of Pale', 'Paint It Black', 'Nights In White Satin', etc.) with hand-picked vocalists.

From the lush orchestral opening of brass and violins through the acoustic guitar/singer-songwriter stylings of the main theme to the almost apocalyptic final quarter, this is undoubtedly a startling entry in Lemmy's songbook. The sound of Pink Floyd-style backing vocalists is both bizarre and intriguing. Whether the sweet juxtaposition of the crooning female voices mixed with Lemmy's sandpaper growl is a good thing is entirely up to you. The whole song has grandeur and sensitivity and the fragility of the main vocal is entirely fitting for the prophetic subject matter.

'Highway To Hell' (Scott/Young/Young)

A.N.I.M.A.L.. Recorded: May 1999. Found on: Usa Toda Tu Fuerza (CD)

Argentinean nu-metal band A.N.I.M.A.L., who usually sing in Spanish, were regular touring partners with Motörhead in Latin America and, while the band were recording an album, they hooked up with Lemmy in a Californian studio to create this blistering take on the AC/DC stalwart. The song is about the incessant touring of the rock lifestyle and it could not be more apt for Lemmy. The band play the tune with few embellishments and little deviation (well, if it's perfect, to begin with, what's the point in messing with it?), although it is far heavier than the original and the ending is a variation on the thrashing sturm and drang concert finale, which suggests it was recorded more or less live. The shared vocals are inimitably gravelly and well-suited to the song, with Lemmy contributing rasping verses and forceful singing on the choruses and ad-libs. They clearly enjoyed themselves breaking out from their usual musical strictures and Lemmy obviously had enormous pleasure singing this timeless song.

'Enter Sandman' (Kirk Hammett/James Hetfield/Lars Ulrich)
Lemmy. Recorded: 1999. Found on: Lemmy: Damage Case (CD)
Mega Motörhead fans, Metallica had covered four of their songs on an EP they christened *Motörheadache*. Lemmy returned the favour more than once, but on this occasion, his vocals are merely serviceable rather than inspired. The strain on his voice is noticeable. Astonishingly this version was nominated for a Grammy in 2000. This was to have been an all Motörhead cover but, due to scheduling issues, the only contributor from the band was Lemmy and he was unable to add his signature bass playing. Instead, alt-metal band, Zebrahead provided a complete musical backing track over which Lemmy could attempt to sing. The difference is clear from the outset as the long-lasting group play the notes and make a heroic stab at the riffs and the tune, but the atmosphere, mood and especially the charm are lacking. The music is virtually a carbon copy of the original but not quite as well produced and the solos are disappointingly flat compared to the original.

Bafflingly this was recorded for an ECW (Extreme Championship Wrestling) compilation album as a theme tune for pro-wrestler The Sandman. What it did achieve was to get Motörhead noticed in the world of World Wrestling Federation music and it would give them a remarkable parallel career path over the next few years.

More recordings
The next project that caught Lemmy's attention was another Elvis tribute, this time instigated by Slim Jim Phantom (of successful throwback rockabilly band The Stray Cats) and Danny B Harvey (of rockabilly revivalists The Rockats). Initially, this involved recording three songs for an album billed as The Swing Cats. Lemmy would sing and play acoustic guitar and there would be various other guests littered throughout the album. When it came to recording the songs, Lemmy, Slim and Danny discovered they had a mutual admiration of the songs of Elvis and other rock and roll icons of the 1950s. While they did record three songs for the original album, they also went on to tape another sixteen songs at further sessions. Enough, it was felt, for an album billed as *Lemmy, Slim Jim and Danny B*. They added two of the three Swing Cats tracks (the other also featured Johnny Ramone on guitar, so was deemed off-limits) to the album and Lemmy found himself in a second, albeit part-time, band! Retrospectively the album was re-christened *Fool's Paradise* in 2006 and reissued with a truncated track-listing under the name The Head Cat, a band with whom Lemmy would tour sporadically in his time off from Motörhead. Given the recording conditions, this sounds like well-played rehearsal fare rather than fully produced takes, but it is better than

bootleg quality and it has some fun moments. The lack of Lemmy on bass is keenly felt.

One of Slim Jim Phantom's quirks is that he is one of that very rare breed: a stand-up drummer – and it led to a quite different live presence for the trio.

We Are Motörhead (Steamhammer/SPV/CMC, May 2000)

Personnel:
Lemmy Kilmister: vocals, bass
Phil Campbell: guitars
Mikkey Dee: drums
Produced at Karo Studios, Germany and American Recorders, California, June-August 1999 and December 1999-March 2000 by Motörhead, Bob Kulick, Bruce Bouillet and Duane Baron.
Highest chart place: UK: 91
Running time (approximate): 38:20

After the debacle of the *Snake Bite Love* recordings, the blame was ultimately laid at the door of erstwhile producer Howard Benson and he was not considered when the band began writing for their next opus. Instead, they opted for three co-producers who had a track record; Duane Baron was well-known for producing *No More Tears*, while Bob Kulick and Bruce Bouillet were production stalwarts. Noting the crucial lead-in times that scuppered their last disc, on this occasion, the band insisted that they got sufficient rehearsal time to hone their recently written songs.

'See Me Burning' (Campbell/Dee/Kilmister)

It's like Mikkey is building up when the drums first come in. Having wound himself up with the initial introduction, the full band scream in with a speedily fast riff and some serious weight. This is the heaviest of metal, which still manages to recall their stated purpose of playing rock and roll at 1000 miles an hour.

There is nothing special in the lyrics (Lemmy wants to bed another conquest) and the chorus is very poor, but the riff melody is addictive and the drumming is a treat.

'Slow Dance' (Campbell/Dee/Kilmister)

A grinding riff is battered by some thick drum work and a rolling tempo, probably ideal for dancing at the end of a night. The chorus is fascinating for being both catchy and repetitive (saying the title several times becomes mesmerising with Lemmy's melodious vocal style), but the verses are inane.

The solo emulates the twin guitar harmonics of Thin Lizzy and Judas Priest at their finest, but it adorns a song that it doesn't quite fit and the stuttered ending is a mistake for this tune.

'Stay Out Of Jail' (Campbell/Dee/Kilmister)

The meaning of these lyrics emerges as the song develops. This is another rumination on the perils of heroin and the plight of addicts. Set to a searing and uncomplicated riff and backed with a rhythm section that is locked in

113

step, this has all the hallmarks of a classic. The tune, the chorus and the vocal melody are all exemplary and the ease with which this appears to have been put together is in stark contrast to the preceding album (and even the earlier songs here). The musical dips that occur just before certain lines are sung is inspired.

'God Save The Queen' (Paul Cook/Steve Jones/John Lydon/Glen Matlock)

Motörhead make their best attempt at this of-its-time punk anthem, but the result is sadly lacking in excitement or innovation. Apparently recorded because the band were great friends with LA-based guitarist Steve Jones, this is one cover version that should have been left for the post-Motörhead compilation *Under Cover* rather than gaining lead single status, as it did for this album. The reason for the song's inclusion can be gleaned from the short run time of the album and the miserable nine self-penned tunes that are here. Without this extra nugget of nonsense, the album could have legitimately been described as an EP. The video for the single was filmed on an open-top London bus in a peculiar homage to the original not-quite promotional appearance by the Sex Pistols on a boat on the Thames. On the plus side, Motörhead weren't arrested when they stepped off the bus, unlike the Sex Pistols and their entourage. It all seems horribly desperate somehow.

'Out To Lunch' (Campbell/Dee/Kilmister)

There is a feeling of déjà vu the moment this song begins. While the riff is different, this sounds like a carbon copy of 'See Me Burning' in its tempo, although it has a better chorus and a distinctly retro rock and roll guitar tone to the solo that actually lifts the song.

Lyrically there is little to excite the listener (it seems to be a series of previous clichés juggled around) and it suggests the lyricist was out to lunch when the words were scrawled down. Lemmy often said that he gave his best lyrics to other bands and, in this instance, he wasn't kidding.

'Wake The Dead' (Campbell/Dee/Kilmister)

A quick glance at the words brings hope to the listener. This is a melancholy reflection on living, the inevitability of death and the people who occupy your time with trivia and nonsense. Strapped to a bare-chested riff and some busy drumming, this rolls along with great aplomb and a slightly complicated structure (where the chorus is identified by the music that backs it rather than by the words used). For some reason, another space is created for a drum solo (presumably intended directly for the live environment) in the middle eight, so the crunch of the return to the main riff is a welcome diversion.

This was probably written as a showcase for Mikkey and, on those terms, it succeeds. The song itself would have benefited from losing the soft solo section, though.

'One More Fucking Time' (Campbell/Dee/Kilmister)

You can't ignore a title like that and the tune is as insistent as the title. It reads like another tale of a partner doing you wrong, but it has a certain rough beauty in the words and an electric guitar figure that captures the imagination. The lilting ballad form is utilised well here and the band make far better use of the form than previously. This seems to be autobiographical in nature (and probably the result of an argument with his long term on-off girlfriend) and it really has an earthy resonance that other ballads in their catalogue lack, which is complemented by a soaring solo from Phil that almost reaches into Dave Gilmour territory.

'Stagefright/Crash & Burn' (Campbell/Dee/Kilmister)

The title makes this look like another song collision, but this cautionary tale of life on the road was conceived as a single song. Combining a patently dirty metal riff with a decidedly punk spirit, this relatively short and brutal thrash is an unexpected highlight. Lemmy even gets to honour his comedy heroes with the first line: 'Flying Circus on the road' and ties it into the subject he really wants to talk about. Phil's squealing solo is a little ear-splitting but very swift, while the end repeat of 'crash and burn' could have been excised, but that's a small quibble when we are presented with this fun concoction.

'(Wearing Your) Heart On Your Sleeve' (Campbell/Dee/Kilmister)

A full and frank lyric graces this surprisingly tempered and well-argued dissection of politics. The chorus is a call to stand up for ourselves and ignore the politicians and, instead, we should trust our own hearts. It is the way Lemmy lived his life, after all. He is baring his soul on this one, complete with swearing.

Against a scorching backing that matches the vituperation of the words, this, almost incidentally, demonstrates how world-class this rhythm section were. Patented bass on the chorus, astonishing drumming throughout and as tight as a wire garrotte, these two were extraordinary when they clicked together. The drumming exhibits the precise and technical nature of heavy metal but lacks the swing of jazz or rhythm and blues, preferring to batter the listener into submission with controlled power.

There's an echo of 1991's 'The One To Sing The Blues' in the tune and the vocal melody, but that's no bad thing. This certainly makes up for the variable material previously heard and it leads nicely into the final track.

'We Are Motörhead' (Campbell/Dee/Kilmister)

This delightfully tongue-in-cheek self-aggrandisement contains a truly hilarious punchline and a bravura sense of braggadocio that is clearly meant in jest. It is a glorious end to the album and it leaves the listener with a grin on their face. How it didn't become a live stalwart, either opening or closing the set, is a mystery.

A signature bass line introduces an 'Ace Of Spades' inspired riff that sounds even scuzzier than its ancestor and the trio rocket through the tune in a punk-inspired frenzy. What a cracking finale to a somewhat wayward album.

Related recordings
'Call to Arms' (Ernest Boetz)
Boetz. Recorded: March 2000. Found on: Call To Arms (CD)
Throwing in a raggedly high vocal from Boetz for the opening verse and the outro chorus, this is an odd combination. There's an almost Red Hot Chili Peppers bounce to the tune and more than a hint of AC/DC in the sonic soundscape, but the whole thing sounds rather like the vocals were added as an afterthought to the guitar work that is on offer here. Nothing wrong with that, especially when Lemmy gives his all with an increasingly croaky top register, but the song attempts to subvert the usual song structure with a verse-verse-solo-verse/middle eight-chorus format which is as perplexing as it sounds and gives the tune a decidedly wonky charm. Basic hard rock and roll and heavy metal don't usually go in for complications of this nature (although there are honourable exceptions like Iron Maiden, Dream Theater and Opeth) and Boetz is not in the same league, or aiming at the same audience as these landmark bands.

'Desire' (Kilmister/Osbourne/Wylde)
Lemmy. Recorded: March 2000. Found on: Bat Head Soup: Tribute To Ozzy (CD)
Following the Motörhead version of 'Hellraiser', Lemmy was asked to sing his own lyric for an Ozzy tribute album, backed this time by seasoned session musicians. This take on the song is very similar to the version on *No More Tears* and was produced by Bruce Bouillet and Bob Kulick around the *We Are Motörhead* sessions (although Phil and Mikkey are noticeable by their absence). It would not be the last time these gentlemen called on Lemmy to provide vocals on cover versions (and more, there's a Christmas song on the way!).

It has the classic Ozzy sound and the playing is very much in keeping with the original; only the singing veers wildly from the previously recorded version. Lemmy makes a good fist of it, but the clean and bright backing track is significantly at odds with his gruff, alcohol-soaked vocal.

'Jumpin' Jack Flash' (Mick Jagger/Keith Richards)
Motörhead. Recorded: March 2000. Found on: Under Cover (CD)
Recorded for an unreleased tribute album, this was ultimately used as a bonus track for the re-released *Bastards* album and used the same production team as 'Desire', although this featured the full Motörhead trio. It is a surprisingly faithful rendition, inevitably given a harder metal edge, and the band acquit themselves well. Phil roughs up the guitars and Mikkey attempts to emulate the remarkable and deceptively uncomplicated jazz swing of Charlie Watts,

although he doesn't quite achieve his goal. It ends up as a fair version that reflects well on the trio but doesn't have quite the verve of the original.

'Alone Again' (Kilmister)
Doro. Recorded: March 2000. Found on: Calling The Wild (limited edition CD)
Written specifically for Doro, this was a duet ballad companion to the version of 'Love Me Forever' that graced the main album.

Vocally the two singers sing almost the entire song together, often harmonised and sparingly multi-tracked, while Lemmy plays the acoustic guitar (including the solo) underneath. It would be fascinating to hear this as a solo Lemmy recording, but it would sound very bare without the Doro band embellishments. There is a tastefully used keyboard and then there is the inevitable power ballad full band crunch during Lemmy's solo, but it is low in the mix and it reinforces the melancholic nature of the song. The electric guitar solo that accompanies the final fade is both restrained and affecting.

'Hardcore' (Dee Snider)
Lemmy. Recorded: May 2001. Found on: Music From The Motion Picture Frezno Smooth (CD)
Twisted Sister were surprisingly successful in the 1980s. Visually a curious New York Dolls/hair metal hybrid, but musically, they were a kind of Slade-meets-Alice Cooper-meets-The Sex Pistols combination that mightily appealed to Lemmy. As he usually did, Lemmy looked past the image and listened to the songs. In this case, he had to, as Dee Snider had, parenthetically, called it 'Hardcore (Lemmy's Song)' when it was first recorded by his solo band on *Never Let The Bastards Wear You Down* (2000). Lemmy was duly taken by this blatant ploy and covered it in style for the film *Frezno Smooth* (2001), a freeway collision of a movie that died a death.

The song, however, streaks along at a punk-infused pace and never lets up and it sounds like a lost Motörhead classic in every department. Lyrically it is a study of Lemmy's life in music and it cheekily quotes Lemmy back to himself in the most affectionate way. Well worth searching out, this is a fantastic cover that could do with far more exposure.

Hammered (Steamhammer/SPV, April 2002)

Personnel:
Lemmy Kilmister: vocals, bass
Phil Campbell: guitars
Mikkey Dee: drums
Produced at Henson Studios and Chuck Reed's House, Los Angeles, November-December 2001 by Thom Panunzio and Motörhead except 'Serial Killer' produced and mixed by Thom Panunzio, Chuck Reed and Lemmy.
Highest chart place: UK: Did Not Chart
Running time (approximate): 41:19

Gearing up for their next recording, Phil and Mikkey flew into LA on 10th September 2001 to join Lemmy in writing and rehearsing a brace of new songs to unleash upon the world. The day after, planes were flown into the twin towers in New York and CIA headquarters in Langley, Virginia. The days that followed were filled with fear and anxiety around the globe. 9/11 has become infamous and, whilst the band was nowhere near the epicentre, the atmosphere inevitably permeated the whole mood of the recording.

'Walk A Crooked Mile' (Campbell/Dee/Kilmister)
Lemmy recalled a very old nursery rhyme (which he consciously references as a means to describe the slippery nature of politicians and psychopaths) from his own youth:

There was a crooked man, and he walked a crooked mile
He found a crooked sixpence against a crooked stile
He bought a crooked cat, which caught a crooked mouse
And they all lived together in a little crooked house

The lyricist ruminates on the dichotomies inherent in the stance of the 9/11 villains and attempts to make some kind of sense of the essentially senseless acts. Directly influenced by an anti-communist film noir of the same name from 1948 (which adds a further layer of meaning), the words paint an impressionistic picture of how askew the world had become at that time. It would get worse, but Lemmy would only see some of it: the political lurch to the Right was often in his sights; however, he wouldn't live to see the days of President Trump and the lame insurrection that accompanied his dismissal from office.

Strapped to a loping beat and with a prominent bass placed high in the mix, this rumbles along nicely, although the chorus vocals seem unlikely to be particularly well reproduced live (Lemmy sings over himself and the lines are echoed out of phase just to make it impossible for a single person to sing), but it doesn't detract from the song at all. It ends with a long and rather nicely restrained solo from Phil before fading out.

'Down The Line' (Campbell/Dee/Kilmister)

Essentially reflecting Lemmy's endlessly restless spirit, this is basically a break-up song where the writer blames himself ('it's not you, it's me'), knowing that they are messing up a good thing. Phil provides a stirring heavy metal/rock and roll riff hybrid and, while the song doesn't have the earworm catchiness that would elevate it to classic status, this is a solid and dependable tune that is worthy of repeated listens. The guitar solo is well done, with the effects pedals working hard, while Phil obviously spent some time perfecting it.

'Brave New World' (Campbell/Dee/Kilmister)

Aldous Huxley's remarkable and prescient novel is given the Lemmy treatment, reflecting on the dystopian nature of the book seventy years later with a look at current society. There is a good deal of 9/11 angst and cynicism towards all governments visible here. Looking back, Lemmy said: 'It seems that our brave new world is becoming less tolerant, spiritual and educated than it ever was when I was young.'

These themes come out clearly in the lyrics and the message is that the novel was alarmingly and disappointingly accurate in some of its predictions. Lemmy fits a lot of words onto this tune and he does it well.

Coupled with the squalling riff and bludgeoning rhythm is a clean and melodic guitar line that raises the musical game and gives the song an unusual hook. The solo is brief but telling and the whole thing races past in a flash that belies its four-minute runtime. Only the basic chorus lets the side down.

'Voices From The War' (Campbell/Dee/Kilmister)

Musing on the afterlife of warriors throughout time, the lyrics are an indignant meditation on the idea that soldiers killed in battle will never rest easy. Lemmy gets lyrical and contemplative here and he does not waste a word. The lyrics are both emotive and extremely well-chosen.

Musically they are shackled to roaring rock bombast and a gut-wrenching riff that conjures images of hand-to-hand fighting and the pointless waste of life. Lemmy opts for a visceral spoken word section as a middle eight, suggesting that the dead will haunt those who now stand upon their sacrifice, which ends with cackling laughter and a return to the main tune. Now Phil adds little guitar shards to almost every line, which adds impact and leads to the unusually melodic feedback fade.

'Mine All Mine' (Campbell/Dee/Kilmister)

Returning to one of his favourite topics, this is Lemmy's interpretation of a romantic boy-meets-girl song. It's a fair lyric, but no more, and is the first sign that he is running out of subject matter and inspiration for the words. Phil provides a serrated rock and roll riff, while Dizzy Reed contributes sparkling piano lower in the mix. This is the sort of song that Motörhead can write in their sleep, and sometimes it sounds like they are sleep-walking through a tune, but this time they give their all and the result is far more fun than the lyrics would imply.

'Shut Your Mouth' (Campbell/Dee/Kilmister)

From the recycled opening riff, this sounds like space-filler with its chunky rhythm, single-note keyboard padding and tired soloing. To balance against that, the words have had some work done on them, but the end result is less than the sum of its parts. The pre-chorus call and response recalls previous attempts at this structure, which also failed.

In hindsight, the band was ambiguous about this album, recognising several strong songs but admitting that there were a few poor compositions. This is undoubtedly one of those.

'Kill The World' (Campbell/Dee/Kilmister)

Curiously this has an Ozzy vibe to its lyrics, although it has never been noted as something that Lemmy proffered to him. The heavy metal riff and sharp drumming add to this impression, although the singing instantly marks this out as Motörhead. Smeared with effects, the solo is far more rock and roll psychedelia than heavy metal cleanliness and brutality.

There's a nice chorus on show, which would suit Ozzy's range and a (somewhat buried, admittedly) melodic sense that brings the song up a notch.

'Doctor Love' (Campbell/Dee/Kilmister)

Perhaps the second part of Lemmy's Doctor trilogy, this particular song concerns the protagonist's rampant desire for a woman he has just seen at a party and the chat up that he uses, boasting of his sexual prowess and claiming he is 'Doctor Love'. It's hardly sophisticated, but it reflects the personality of the writer. It also seems to have been inspired by the KISS song 'Calling Dr Love' as Lemmy slips in a cheeky reference or two to it in his reliably humorous lyrics.

Lemmy gives us his almost-spoken double-tracked chorus vocal, although he sings the verses and ends on a lascivious reading of the title. The words and music work well together, which has not always been the case, and the brevity of the song is a bonus as it does not outstay its welcome.

'No Remorse' (Campbell/Dee/Kilmister)

Readers will recognize the title here, but it's a very belated (18 years!) title track for the 1984 compilation. Concentrating deliberately on Christian mythology because Lemmy was less acquainted with other religions, this draws a clear parallel with the Al-Qaeda belief that martyrs will end up in Heaven. The unequivocal lyrical riposte is: 'If you believe these tales they tell, Then you deserve to burn in Hell'.

The music is a rolling grinding riff, in an almost Black Sabbath vein, that could run forever. The solo has a quirky charm that suggests Tony Iommi is being mugged by John Frusciante in a playful mood. It all fades out on a squealing second solo that adds to the grimly bleak tone.

'Red Raw' (Campbell/Dee/Kilmister)
There are plenty of lyrical allusions to vampires and serial killers here, which have the name Jack the Ripper hovering uncomfortably overhead. The grisly lyrics and grand Guignol atmosphere are juxtaposed by the frantic punk thrash of the music, which illustrates the frenzied killing that takes place but misses any of the subtlety that might have been deployed.

In one sense, it is merely an introductory piece to the forthcoming finale, which takes a very different musical route. Here the chorus is barely distinguishable from the verses and the whole song seems to be a race to see who can reach the end fastest. Popping in the sound effect of an explosion seems redundant given the pummelling noise that preceded it.

'Serial Killer' (Kilmister)
Attempting, and failing to recapture the sonic depths of 'Orgasmatron', while continuing the visceral horror tone, this is half an idea stretched beyond its limit (and it's less than two minutes long!). Sadly it is a little more *Carry On Screaming* than *Saw*. Almost entirely unmusical (there's squealing feedback and sparse drumming) and mostly spoken rather than sung, it trumpeted a vocal duet with pro-wrestler Triple H, but he is only visible on the final verse, low in the mix, and the screeching pounding backing is cut dead to finish proceedings on a decidedly disappointing note.

Related recordings
'The Game' (James Johnston)
Motörhead. Recorded: February 2001. Found on: Everything Louder Forever (CD)
The presence of Triple H on the main album is explained by this specially written anthem that introduced him on many World Wrestling bouts. The writer of the song has created numerous tunes for various wrestlers and often, they are performed by rock bands of pedigree (e.g. Monster Magnet). Motörhead carved out a separate niche career with these theme tunes; this is the first of three recordings they made. All of them should have been compiled onto an album of genuinely rare Motörhead songs.

Playing to the audience, there is a great swaggering stride to this that makes it perfect entrance music. There is a subtle synthesizer presence and a ridiculously flamboyant double solo that should bring a smile to any listener's face. Adding in the ad-libbed maniacal laughter and the remarkable glee of the vocals, this confident strut of a song is a delightful heavy rock anthem that sits a little outside the main Motörhead catalogue but deserves to be given far wider exposure, which it finally gets on the career-spanning compilation *Everything Louder Forever*.

'Shoot 'Em Down' (Snider)
Motörhead. Recorded: February 2001. Found on: Under Cover (CD)
Motörhead show their continuing appreciation of Twisted Sister with this
committed and characteristically enjoyable cover. Boasting a heavy rock and
roll heartbeat, the sheer fun that was infecting the band at this time was in
stark contrast to *Hammered*. Lemmy's elation on singing the words 'mass
debater' is made clearer with his vocal high in the mix at that point. The trio
relishes the opportunity and has a whale of a time playing the song and its
position on *Under Cover* is assured, proving a highlight on that otherwise
somewhat thin collection.

'Rockaway Beach' (Dee Dee Ramone)
Motörhead. Recorded: June 2002. Found on: Under Cover (CD)
Another peak is this affectionate and rambunctious punk thrash through
a tune that the whole band adored. Lemmy was a huge Ramones fan but
didn't need to persuade the guys to record this far-from-throwaway rock
and roll demo at the *Hammered* sessions. It was left unmixed at the time
when it wasn't required to serve as a b-side, a bonus track or a tribute
album contribution (odd, given that Johnny Ramone and Rob Zombie
curated a Ramones tribute album, *We're A Happy Family*, in 2003 which
featured Red Hot Chili Peppers, Metallica, KISS, U2, Garbage and Marilyn
Manson amongst many others). However, it was given a nice bit of spit and
polish fifteen years later by Cameron Webb for its eventual release on *Under
Cover* as the only other unreleased recording and it adds class to that sparse
compilation.

'Thirsty & Miserable' (Des Cadena/Rose Medea/Robo)
Lemmy. Recorded: August 2002. Found on: Rise Above: 24 Black Flag Songs to
Benefit the West Memphis Three (CD)
This song is from a benefit album for the West Memphis 3, three teenagers
convicted of a triple murder of three boys in 1994. There were several TV
documentaries in America that throw widespread doubt on the validity of the
convictions, although the men were only released in 2011, having served 18
years of their sentences. Due to the complex nature of their release agreement,
they are technically both innocent and guilty.

Henry Rollins organised and produced a benefit album in 2002, which had
songs by Black Flag, all played by the Rollins Band, with a variety of guest
vocalists enlisted.

Musically this is walloping hardcore punk with a truly individual bass player
and a guitarist who enjoys dissonance.Lemmy graces the tune with rock-solid
vocals and an attitude that speaks volumes about his commitment to punk
and the teenagers (who appear to have been tried in part because of their
musical taste).

'One Way Love' (Martin Kent/Kilmister)

Ace Sounds. Recorded: February 2003. Found on: Still Hungry (CD)
This is guitarist Ace from Skunk Anansie, who was recording his debut
solo album and managed to catch Lemmy in L.A. for a few days to get his
songwriting input. It might be imagined that this was outside of Lemmy's
musical field, but he was captivated by the underlying tune and wrote a striking
lyric and provided a fine vocal performance to top it off.

The introduction is a twisting guitar line (although it has distinct synthesizer
tinges) and the production exposes a definite early Skunk Anansie lilt to it,
undoubtedly because three-quarters of that band contribute to this particular
song, Lemmy restricting himself to singing on this barnstormer. Ace throws
in a welter of guitar sounds and effects (including his attempt to sound like a
police siren in the solo) onto a mid-tempo chassis that suits Lemmy down to
his bespoke boots.

'Shake Your Blood' (Dave Grohl/Kilmister)

Probot. Recorded: March 2001. Found on: Probot (CD)
There's an overwhelming feeling that this could be a lost Eddie-era Motörhead
classic, just recorded 20 years too late and consequently a smidge heavier.
Lemmy adds his signature bass and vocals to this deep cut tune which grows in
stature on each playing. Grohl plays his heart out on both guitars and drums
and ends up with a winning song that could happily have graced *Ace of Spades*
without comment. The drumming has more of a Mikkey weight and feel to
it, rather than Philthy, but otherwise, this is 1980 all over again. Grohl claims
Lemmy completed his contributions in two takes and the spontaneity and
vigour of the song attest to that.

'Shout It Out Loud' (Bob Ezrin/Gene Simmons/Paul Stanley)

Lemmy. Recorded: February 2004. Found on: Spin The Bottle: An All-Star Tribute to
KISS (CD)
Two of the production team for *Hammered* came up with another tribute
album and persuaded Lemmy to sing and play bass on this extroverted cover.
Backed by Jennifer Batten on guitars, Samantha Maloney on drums and a duo
of whiskey-voiced backing singers, this is a startlingly vivacious homage to the
larger-than-life pop-metal charmers and their chorus-heavy catchiness.

The musicians tackle the song with a verve and attack that indicates a
genuine love for KISS and they provide one of the true standouts to the *Spin
The Bottle* album. Lemmy sounds as though he is having fun even when his
vocals strain in the higher registers demanded.

Inferno (Steamhammer/SPV/Sanctuary, June 2004)

Personnel:
Lemmy Kilmister: vocals, bass, acoustic guitar, harmonica
Phil Campbell: guitars, backing vocals
Mikkey Dee: drums
Steve Vai: guest guitars
Curtis Mathewson: Strings
Produced at NRG, Paramount and Maple Studios, Los Angeles, February-March 2004 by Cameron Webb.
Highest chart place: UK: 95
Running time (approximate): 50:58

Just to add to Lemmy's extra-curricular CV, he began recording his debut solo album, *Lemmy And Friends*, for fun during his time off. Additional songs were recorded during sessions with Dave Grohl and Skew Siskin and further collaborations would be recorded over the next ten years. There are songs he completed with The Damned, Reverend Horton Heat and others in the can, but he never managed the duet with Janet Jackson as he had hoped.

The time appeared right for the band to ring the changes in the production department for their next album and the insistent Cameron Webb seemed the obvious choice, even if he offended Lemmy on their first meeting by effectively calling them a Heavy Metal band. Nevertheless, he was hired for the job and the band were so impressed that they would place the rest of their recorded career in his hands, even for posthumous releases. In this instance, he also produced their heaviest ever album.

'Terminal Show' (Campbell/Dee/Kilmister)

The sheer force of the full band attack that opens the album sets out the stall for the dozen songs that follow. Motörhead are as ferocious as the hungriest young band on the block and they are in no mood to take prisoners. On top of Phil's raging riff, legendary guitar virtuoso Steve Vai lays down treble-heavy lead guitar and a frankly intimidatingly fast solo. The bass occupies much the same frequencies as the lead guitar, so it is left to the rhythm guitar and the bass drums to cover the bottom end of the spectrum.

Meanwhile, Lemmy growls his thoughts of impending death in a grim fantasy world analogy of blind kings and red queens that recalls *Game of Thrones* at its bloodiest. These are patently not first draft lyrics as the scansion, rhyming and internal logic are all immaculate.

'Killers' (Campbell/Dee/Kilmister)

Cranking up another blazing riff, and this time giving the busy bass some audio room, this slows the pace slightly while adding in little pockets of light and shade to rough up the otherwise identikit song progression. There is a rock and roll backbeat poking through the heavy blanket, which immediately identifies it as Motörhead and, while the melody is straightforward, there is little sign of overt catchiness – just the sound of a sterling album track.

The lyrics again inhabit a realm of fear, death and chaos; the overarching theme is of the senselessness of war and conflict in whichever age the words reference.

'In The Name Of Tragedy' (Campbell/Dee/Kilmister)

Matt Sorum had to play this for a live tour by the band, and singled it out as a highlight for a drummer and remarked on how detailed and complex the rhythms were from Mikkey. It again starts with the trio blasting into the stratosphere before easing off the pedal for the verses and then tripling the weight of the music for the brutal choruses and stinging solo.

The vocal melody reflects the driving force of the music and, again, fits the blistering backing with the pessimistic words adding a serious topping. There are moments over the album where Lemmy slurs his words or appears too far from the microphone for it to pick up every nuance.

'Suicide' (Campbell/Dee/Kilmister)

A relatively standard riff punts this song into a mid-tempo chug which has a quirky and catchy chorus (where the vocal harmonies and double-tracking come into their own) and the third verse has an almost completely different melody, just to show that Motörhead are well able to innovate even within their own self-imposed restrictions. It doubles as a middle-eight, except that it is then repeated for the final and lengthy guitar solo, which eventually fades the song out. The solo itself is somewhat uninspired, but that's more than made up for by the melodic patches of singing.

The words look at environmental collapse and the apparent lemming instinct of human beings who won't admit that they are basically committing suicide in the way they use up the Earth's finite resources.

It is all summed up in the chorus:

No sun just clouds and poison rain
Raped and freezing
Victims of the Dream again

'Life's A Bitch' (Campbell/Dee/Kilmister)

In 1999 Lemmy wrote the lyrics for a song by Skew Siskin with the same title. The phrase obviously appealed to him as he pulled out a new set of words to go with the sturdy rock and roll tune that the band came up with here. Although the song works well as an album cut, it lacks the hook that would raise it above the mid-range in Motörhead terms. When the tune ends with that hoary cliché of the live ending thrash about, it's neither a surprise nor an improvement. This is the one set of words on this album that seem thrown together at the last minute.

'Down On Me' (Campbell/Dee/Kilmister)

Steve Vai turns in a stunning and dissonant end solo which sums up the rocket-fuelled riffery on display. A hint of heavy metal production and a bludgeoning rhythm section guarantee the metal audience a great time, while the punk inflections in both the singing and the solid chorus cater for other needs. Lemmy gets unexpectedly romantic in the final chorus because he was in a relationship at the time:

> Give your hands to hold me
> Give your arms to enfold me
> Say the word set me free
> Bring me in, out from the storm
> Keep me safe from scorn
> Down on me
> Down on me

'In The Black' (Campbell/Dee/Kilmister)

Making use of a bank balance metaphor, Lemmy looks at the positive side of the relationship he was in at the time. Swearing that he 'can't go back, can't go back, can't be who I was back then' and promising to rescue her if she should 'fall in the ocean' and he would 'scramble through the wreckage, to keep you safe from harm,' this is a side to Lemmy that is seldom seen (and even rarer when he writes about it). Someone is definitely occupying his tender thoughts.

Hooking his heart-on-sleeve words to a stirring chorus and a cracking riff from Phil carries the song through right to the end and even the pantomime solo break gives the song a joyful bounce that cannot be denied. Probably unrepeatable live, the chorus vocals switch back sharply and effortlessly while the Metallica-inspired ending rounds off a catchy yet heavy brute of a song.

'Fight' (Campbell/Dee/Kilmister)

No one will be shocked that this is all about conflict but what might raise an eyebrow is the simple repetition that occurs throughout. We are greeted with the deathless cry, 'put the bass up, will ya!' which begins this speed metal dash for the finish line. Mikkey again demonstrates his unerring chops and sheer power on this blunt force tune.

This song was always destined to become a live favourite so why it was so infrequently played is a mystery. Along with that surprise is the knowledge that Motörhead toured with Rob Halford's intense speed/thrash metal group Fight in the 1990s and that was an inspiration for the words.

'In The Year Of The Wolf' (Campbell/Dee/Kilmister)

Although ostensibly about being a werewolf, the deeper meaning is visible; the subtext is that the narrator was a predatory animal looking for instant gratification, all the while hunting for a deeper, stronger relationship with another person. The vocals make the best of the metaphor, sounding both lascivious and blood-drenched, while the musical accompaniment is fierce and memorable.

'Keys To The Kingdom' (Campbell/Dee/Kilmister)
Kicking in with a rolling lope and a vigorous riff, there's a catchy tone to the tune that cannot be denied; the lyrics portray a rather more pessimistic outlook. Phil shows a nice line in melodic chorus work and a striking solo, while the presence of strings on the chorus provides a subliminal lift to the musicality already on show.

The lyrics appear to err on the side of pessimism but don't always follow a train of thought, the words being used for effect rather than meaning:

King of frustration, Vampire de Luxe
Keys to the Kingdom, God hates your guts

'Smiling Like A Killer' (Campbell/Dee/Kilmister)
It is difficult to tell if Lemmy is being serious with these lyrics, so, knowing his sense of humour, he clearly thinks these words are an absolute hoot. Using the standard horror film tropes and clichés, he fashions a film treatment of stage directions from the point of view of the insane mass murderer. Pick any horror icon (Jason, Freddy, etc.) and spot the allusions (though the mask used in *Scream* is the most apparent progenitor).

Attached to a four-piece Motörhead riff and featuring an over-the-top solo, the band prove that there is still room for fun in their peculiar world, all the while hinting at the memorable riff first used in 'R.A.M.O.N.E.S.'

'Whorehouse Blues' (Campbell/Dee/Kilmister)
Ending on a country blues song with a slightly confrontational lyric is a bold move for a band determined to reassert their place in the musical world. This sounds like it could have been recorded from the 1950s on; it would certainly have formed the cornerstone of the mooted acoustic project that never quite got off the ground.

The aged and gruff delivery suits the pulled-up-by-our-bootstraps story and the reflective reminiscence of the lyrics. Phil proves that he can solo on acoustic as well as electric guitars and that back-porch feeling is completed with Lemmy's striking harmonica playing.

Just to add to the retrospective stance, the song concentrates on the early touring years of the band, although for Lemmy, that might well mean Motörhead post-*Sacrifice*. This is a rather wonderful end to a bare-knuckle hard album which, astonishingly, exhibits a little more maturity than before.

Related recordings
'Line In The Sand (Evolution)' (Johnston)
Motörhead. Recorded: March 2004. Found on: ThemeAddict: The Music V6 (CD)
Boasting another mid-paced lollop, this rare theme tune to a World Wrestling
Faction event would not fit onto the raging *Inferno*. The bite and simple fire
of that album is lost on this melodic hard rock song which, nonetheless, works
very well in context. In a rare move, this was actually produced and mixed
by the songwriter himself, which is why the sonic soundscape is so removed
from the current album, and probably why the song is softer and slower than
the band's recent release. Playing someone else's specially written song can
sometimes be a trial, but Motörhead turn out to be surprisingly adept. There is
a catchy semi-chorus and a creeping melody that insinuates itself like a python
which gives it a great deal of charm.

'Whiplash' (Hetfield/Ulrich)
Motörhead. Recorded: March 2004. Found on: Under Cover (CD)
Motörhead win a Grammy for someone else's song! It sounds pitch-perfect for
Motörhead, though and Lemmy makes it defiantly their own with his lyrical
changes. The tempo is brutally sped up from the original, and the song has a
heaviness that is crushing, which improves it significantly from Metallica's *Kill
'Em All* recording. It would have fitted onto *Inferno* without any qualms; such
is its sheer power. They may not have written it, but this is quintessential and
breathtaking, Motörhead that quashes any talk of the band being has-beens.
This is vital and courageous music from a band that could have rested on their
legacy, but instead, they strive for greater.

'The Trooper' (Steve Harris)
Lemmy and Phil Campbell. Recorded: April 2005. Found on: Lemmy: Damage Case
(CD)
Bob Kulick called the band up for a tour of duty on the *Numbers From
The Beast* tribute recordings and almost managed a Motörhead cover (Phil
and Lemmy are present, but there's no sign of Mikkey, although he drums
elsewhere on the album) of a proper Heavy Metal tune. It retains the
galumphing rhythm and the melody, but Lemmy contributes his own inimitable
vocals and never attempts to emulate Bruce Dickinson's operatic range. In a
surprising move, Lemmy does not play *that* Steve Harris bass part. The thing to
remember is that this is basically the same as the Iron Maiden version but with
a different singer. It is strange that this didn't make it onto the posthumous
Under Cover compilation.

Kiss Of Death (Steamhammer/SPV, August 2006)

Personnel:
Lemmy Kilmister: vocals, bass
Phil Campbell: guitars
Mikkey Dee: drums
C. C. Deville: guest guitar
Mike Inez: guest guitar
Produced at NRG, Paramount and Maple Studios, Los Angeles, March-May 2006 by
Cameron Webb.
Highest chart place: UK: 45
Running time (approximate): 44:54

'Sucker' (Campbell/Dee/Kilmister)
Multi-tracked guitar feedback opens proceedings and then a pulverising
rhythm and a slicing riff are thrown into the mix. This is heavy late-period
Motörhead and it would have fitted on *Inferno* without question. It has a hook-
laden chorus and a short running time which gives it that punk edge and it
crushes all before it. 'Sucker' has echoes of 'Burner' in the way it uses the title,
but this is harder and even more powerful than that.

'One Night Stand' (Campbell/Dee/Kilmister)
Another touring song, and a reflection on much of Lemmy's road life, this
was written while he was still in the same relationship noted on *Inferno*. On
and off, he had a 20-year relationship with the same Afro-American woman
(who, as an aside, was in the 'Whorehouse Blues' video), which started in
1995. How she felt about this ode to the parade of single encounters he had
while performing around the world is unrecorded. He sings unrepentantly
and with a startling catchiness that is signally autobiographical about his
excitement on each occasion. He calls himself a 'slut' in the lyrics and he uses
the term correctly.

The music is a rhythmic romp with a rock and roll heartbeat, allied to a
melodic tune. There is a danger that this will be ignored, given that it has many
similarities with other songs by the band, but the continuing freshness with
which it is presented would make any dismissal unfair.

'Devil I Know' (Campbell/Dee/Kilmister)
Given his way with words, this reads like Lemmy is returning to an argument
with his girlfriend and attempting to gain the upper hand. There is a distinct
edge and bitterness to the lyrics that speak of chewing over old discussions
while acknowledging that he won't be leaving her any time soon.

There is room for a treble-heavy bass solo, unusually, although the musical
chassis again relies on a rock and roll foundation which tends to blur into
similar riffs scattered over the album.

'Trigger' (Campbell/Dee/Kilmister)

With virtually no between-song gap, 'Trigger' slices into view and shows a very different sonic outlook with its 1980s Iron Maiden guitars and solos clamped on to defiantly heavy metal riffs. Apart from the up-to-the-minute production and the curious rhythmic change in the middle eight, this feels like an olde worlde New Wave of British Heavy Metal song just twenty years out of its time. There is even an unmistakable whiff of KISS in the chorus, which, for this song, is no bad thing. Rhyming 'lazy' with 'crazy' is no great feat, but the emphasis put on it in the vocals, and accentuated by the mix, actually gives the track an identity.

'Under The Gun' (Campbell/Dee/Kilmister)

Phil pulls out another loping rock and roll riff from his bag of tricks and anchors this Bonnie and Clyde tale with a plethora of solos (only the last of which, from guest Mike Inez of Alice In Chains, bears scrutiny). Lemmy often said that he preferred slower and more melodic guitar solos while accepting that Phil's tastes were for fast top-string runs. In this instance, Lemmy has it right, as Phil's solos tend to blur together into one screeching mess if he is not reined in. This may explain why there are more guest guitarists featured in future albums.

The tune itself is another triumph and has a chorus lilt that fits the later verses' theme of illicit sex while on the run from the law.

'God Was Never On Your Side' (Campbell/Dee/Kilmister)

Here is another confrontational song in semi-ballad form and it is a huge improvement on previous efforts. Savagely questioning the non-intervention of God and reluctantly seeing it as proof of his non-existence, the lyrics tear into religions of every persuasion and instead place reason at the pinnacle of human evolution. Assuredly this is a weighty topic for a song (and one that has defeated many a songwriter), but the words are both heartfelt and precise here and they ring with the singer's utter conviction. Lemmy adds an individualised vocal to certain words and lines, which only accentuates his investment in the lyrics.

The subtle presence of keyboards is merely there to add bulk to the lower end of the sonic spectrum, while C.C. Deville of Poison drops in a solo to save Phil the effort of thinking up another one.

'Living In The Past' (Campbell/Dee/Kilmister)

Not a cover of the famous Jethro Tull song (which would have been ...interesting) but a pounding indictment of a break-up which has a strangely flattened chorus and a killer riff that maybe needed a different vocal melody laid on top. The verses are practically spoken, so the chorus has more work to do and it isn't up to the task, unfortunately.

It is a shame because that initial riff deserved so much more. The trio can't hit the bulls-eye every time and this is by no means the worst song they have released.

'Christine' (Campbell/Dee/Kilmister)

Lyrically a paean to his girlfriend of the time, this is lasciviousness writ large (and with a sense of humour thrown in). The line 'She moves like a rattlesnake made out of razor blades' may not make a great deal of sense, but the meaning is somehow explicit. Curiously, the track recalls a number of songs named 'Christine' and even the rocky Funkadelic tune 'Red Hot Mama' gets a mention.

The musicians provide a swaying groove that must have got Lemmy's mind racing the moment he heard it, such is the close link between the tune and the words.

'Sword Of Glory' (Campbell/Dee/Kilmister)

A Motörhead album wouldn't be the same without a chugging roar about the futility of war and this is no exception. Many people miss the innate irony in Lemmy's lyrics and titles, particularly outside the U.K., and accuse him of war-mongering when his stance was always diametrically opposed to conflict.

Phil double-tracks his solo, giving it the flavour of Judas Priest, while Mikkey continues to earn his reputation as a heavy hitter. The vocals again feature some really unique phrasing and individualistic moments, which illustrate the care that is still being taken with the songs, even after all these years.

'Be My Baby' (Campbell/Dee/Kilmister)

Far from being a recognisable love song, or even a song about sex, this seems to be a writing exercise set to a bludgeoning rhythm and a grinding riff. The meaning is secondary to the sound the words make. Lemmy's focus on the word 'hardcore' brings his previous cover version to mind, but it is the word 'webcore' that might cause confusion to some. The Webcor (correct spelling) was a very old reel-to-reel tape machine brand that was used for recording in the 1950s and 1960s as it had the remarkable facility to record a full two hours of sound before the tape needed changing. It was, inevitably, used by early rock and roll bands and continued to be used to make demos for many years after.

'Kingdom Of The Worm' (Campbell/Dee/Kilmister)

A deeply malignant lyric swamps this brutal tune which has more in common with extreme metal bands than anything Motörhead had previously come up with. There is no brightness or humour here. This is the sound of defeat set to music, with a nihilistic intensity hitherto unknown. What sparked this vision of darkness and despair is unknown, although the continuing conflicts around the world were certainly on Lemmy's mind.

Phil and Mikkey must have been listening to a lot of doom metal and stoner rock to have brought this forth in the writing sessions. The slightly detuned guitars make that clear as, musically, this has much in common with the riffs of early Black Sabbath. As a departure from their usual template, this is both innovative and unusual, but apparently, no one actually noticed.

'Going Down' (Campbell/Campbell/Dee/Kilmister)

The earliest writing sessions included Todd Campbell's input in the form of a riff which made it to the final version. This is a rather brighter sounding scurry for the finish line which has some wonderful scything guitar and a Formula One speed that finds Lemmy spitting the words out as if he is late for an appointment.

The lyrics are jumbled up song titles strapped to the runaway charge of the rhythm section. It's a great way to end the album, although the repeated riff that finishes the tune may be over-repetitious, with the knowledge that the fire ignited in the band by Cameron Webb shows little sign of burning out.

Related recordings

'King Of Kings' (Johnston)

Motörhead. Recorded: March 2006. Found on: WWE: Wreckless Intent (CD)

The third in their trilogy of World Wrestling anthems, this is a second theme tune for Triple H (for those bouts where 'The Game' is just too introverted and lacking in pomp and self-importance...). Produced during the *Kiss Of Death* sessions, this has Cameron Webb's fingerprints all over it, with its hard-hitting drums, scathing guitars and heavier sonics. It follows the footprints of the two previous contributions by setting the tune firmly in mid-pace territory, but it contains a storming solo from Phil and a monstrous riff. The lyrics are hilariously egotistical and Lemmy sings them with a chortle not far away from his vocal. In many ways, this is the epitome of wrestling as it is extremely entertaining and almost entirely choreographed and tongue-in-cheek. Surely no one takes this seriously?

'Losing You' (Dacia Bridges)

Dacia + the WMD. Recorded: May 2006. Found on: Dacia + the WMD (CD)

Dacia was an American singer who spent a large part of her career being huge in Germany. She died unexpectedly in 2019. She covered many musical genres and found fame in Europe with her band Tape, who combined her powerful R&B vocal qualities with a distinctly hard rock backing. By 2006 she was recording her debut band album, with Ace producing. She felt this song had a Nick Cave and Kylie Minogue 'Where The Wild Roses Grow' vibe and wanted to duet with Lemmy in order to bring out the same contrasts. On this recording, Dacia has a smoky and soulful tone, while Lemmy has that oyster-in-the-pearl grit that is unmistakable.

Musically this has all the hallmarks of an undiscovered Evanescence track, while the tune and vocals follow the familiar pattern of the rock ballad duet, complete with chorus crunches and expressive melodies. Lemmy gives a good account of himself, although his raspy singing is somewhat lower in the mix after his initial verse appearance.

'Back In The USSR' (John Lennon/Paul McCartney)

Lemmy. Recorded: May 2006. Found on: Butchering the Beatles: A Headbanging Tribute (CD)

Notching up another appearance for Bob Kulick, on this occasion for a heavy metal Beatles tribute, this is a good song choice for Lemmy. Ironically this album, too, features all of the current line-up of Motörhead on various songs but without ever putting the three of them together. Instead, we have journeyman drummer Eric Singer (KISS, Black Sabbath, Alice Cooper), industrial rock guitarist John 5 (Marilyn Manson, Rob Zombie) and Lemmy on bass and vocals for this affectionate but steely take on one of the most recognisable tunes in history. Bob adds the Beach Boys-styled backing vocals and the unmistakable sound of heavy metal balalaika (!) to the pot and the whole song brims with a delight and joy that is out of kilter with the somewhat po-faced and serious image of heavy metal that the wider public perceive.

Unfortunately, the results of the lengthy impromptu acoustic gig that Lemmy did at the end of the studio session are omitted. Lemmy was always a huge admirer of The Beatles and he seemed to have committed almost their entire twelve album output to memory. It's a shame no one had the foresight to keep the tape rolling.

'Bad Boyz 4 Life' (Kelly Dunmore/Kilmister)

Keli Raven featuring Lemmy. Recorded: July 2006. Found on: Download only

Lemmy referred to himself and Keli as the 'bad boys for life', but the distinctly dated title must just have seemed like a good idea at the time. Finally able to work together, the result is this surprisingly pop/rock tune that has hints of hip-hop production and Bon Jovi-style commercialism to it. Keli plays all the instruments himself and lays down a funk-influenced base before swathing on layers of guitars. It's a long time before Lemmy gives a vocal appearance, and, in the video, he appears quite uncomfortable on this destined-for-a-b-side Lenny Kravitz wannabe. There is potential here, but the execution leaves something to be desired. No disrespect to Keli, but the song needs more Lemmy and less of the female backing accompaniment.

The reason why this deserves a place in a list of Lemmy's outside collaborations, apart from the fact that he gives a great account of himself on the track itself, is the remarkable afterlife that the song has enjoyed. L.A.-based Cleopatra Records have got hold of the multi-track recordings and passed them on to erstwhile Hawkwind bass player Alan Davey who has radically rebuilt the song to suit different occasions.

Stripping out Lemmy's vocal track, the song was re-tooled to appear in the Cleopatra Films release *Sunset Society* (a vampire movie). For this version, the arrangement was completely upended (with all of Keli's input excised) and the music was re-recorded to produce a decent Motörhead facsimile (complete with Eddie-style guitar flourishes and a perfect imitation of

Lemmy's bass playing by Alan), although there is a rock and roll piano that also chunters along which slightly sets it apart.

Having provided this, admittedly impressive, photocopy of a Motörhead song in 2018, it followed that Alan would attempt another assault on 'Bad Boys For Life' for his Lemmy-era Hawkwind homage, which he has dubbed Hawkestrel. Sure enough, on their debut album, *The Future Is Us* (2019), a radically different reinvention was heard wherein the ghosts of 'Silver Machine' and *Space Ritual* were invoked, although what the bombastic Keith Emerson-lite keyboard solo is doing here is anybody's guess. The vocals are mixed lower, as befits the thick and soupy feel that was desired, and the bass work is actually markedly different to the soundtrack recording, while the additional backing vocals work surprisingly well. It is only the cantering pace, the totally off-piste lyrics and the sore-thumb solo that mark this version out as the ersatz Hawkwind that it is.

The Hawkestrel version is the easiest to purchase, while the other variants are harder to find. On balance, the movie version is the most suited to a book on Motörhead, if you can find it.

Motorizer (Steamhammer/SPV, August 2008)

Personnel:
Lemmy Kilmister: vocals, bass
Phil Campbell: guitars
Mikkey Dee: drums
Wesley Mischener: guest slide guitar
Produced at Studio 606 and Sage & Sound Studios, Los Angeles, December
2007-January 2008 by Cameron Webb.
Highest chart place: UK: 32
Running time (approximate): 38:55

'Runaround Man' (Campbell/Dee/Kilmister)

Not just an attempt to justify sleeping around, this is a rumination on the
problems of maintaining long-distance relationships by telephone from all over
the world. The road life is, by its very nature, nomadic and doesn't leave much
room for partners. Alice Cooper deals with this complication by taking his wife
and children on tour with him (his daughters are his backing singers), but he
remains a rarity in the world of touring rock bands. This commentary is aimed
at Lemmy's ex-girlfriend and it seeks to rationalise the lifestyle he has led for
more than forty years.

A whip-crack snare snaps into a stomping opener, and the only let up from
the relentless pounding is the riff and drum solo masquerading as a middle
eight. It's clear that the band hasn't lost any of their fire or aggression on the
evidence of this song.

'Teach You How To Sing The Blues' (Campbell/Dee/Kilmister)

While the title recalls 'The One To Sing The Blues' from 1991, this is a very
different song in every respect. Marginally dialling down the heaviness from the
previous track, at least until the guitar solo rips through the tune, the riff has
a blunt hook that will please the group's die-hard fans. The lyrical thrust has
the writer berating fashion-obsessed fly-by-night music industry businessmen
and their wily ways. Giving the song three choruses could be confusing, but the
melody remains the same and only the words are rewritten for each chorus.

'When The Eagle Screams' (Campbell/Dee/Kilmister)

Lemmy was quick to point to the Iraq War(s) as the inspiration for these lyrics.
He found himself watching young men going to war to protect oil interests
and, ultimately, money and power. The lyrics argue his case emotively, but
it is based on sound knowledge and forensic, historical study. Lemmy knew
about war, in all its many forms, from his voracious reading and from the many
personal accounts he collected. He should have been awarded an honorary
doctorate for the breadth and depth of his knowledge about historical conflicts.
An intelligent man, he never looked for that kind of accolade; it doesn't take

135

away the fact that he was a self-taught historian of the highest order and he had the insight to back it up.

The musical backing is powerful and controlled, which melds perfectly with the lyrical theme. A spare bass solo is interrupted by a wailing guitar solo that gives a taste of the desperate fear that soldiers can exhibit in battle, simply down to its atypical and somewhat atonal style. Towards the end of the song, Phil deliberately imitates Wurzel's playing style, which may well have sparked the idea for the words.

'Rock Out' (Campbell/Dee/Kilmister)

This is another laugh out loud song for anyone who takes rock and roll too seriously. Admittedly, this is full throttle Motörhead, to be sure but with some of the funniest lyrics ever written. Harking back to the infamous incident when Jim Morrison of The Doors was arrested for apparently 'getting it out on stage' and referencing the hippie musical Hair, which had an entire scene performed in the nude (and that sometimes included the audience!), Lemmy undoubtedly decided to highlight the hedonism and absurdity of the touring rock band lifestyle and these words are the result.

A throbbing bass line opens the song, but, unlike most Motörhead tracks, it remains the dominant instrument throughout this punk-inspired two minutes of fun. Given the treble-heavy tone of the bass, it is extremely hard to differentiate Phil's guitar work, especially when the bass is also the solo instrument.

'One Short Life' (Campbell/Dee/Kilmister)

Musing on his own mortality, the lyrics could well serve as an epitaph for Lemmy. Whether his mother said these little words of wisdom to the young Ian or not, this is clearly autobiographical and sets out how Lemmy lived his life:

> Now even though I'm old and weird
> I remember what she said
> I always knew that she was right
> So I kept it in my head
> I never tried to hurt the world
> I never was drove by greed
> Believe I mostly did my best
> What more do you want from me?

This honest reminiscence is poured out over a roughed up blues tune that fits perfectly, echoing the idea that old wisdom has been brought up-to-date.

'Buried Alive' (Campbell/Dee/Kilmister)

A strangely impenetrable lyric, this has a particularly pessimistic feel which suggests the writer is finding it very hard to cope with the world. Strapping these melancholy words to a rocket ship of a tune is a clever move as it smothers the lyrics with a blanket of noise and speed. Instrumentally every member of the band acquits themselves well and the only disappointment is that the booklet somehow misses out both the third chorus and the fourth verse of the song.

'English Rose' (Campbell/Dee/Kilmister)

Inevitably, the title is used ironically as the lyrics continually refer to a 'nasty girl' in the writer's life. The irony is made explicit in the chorus line: 'English rose, a crown of thorns' and is carried through the whole song.

Lemmy gets to open the song unaccompanied vocally and then rides along with the rock and roll tune that appears out of the ether. The chorus doesn't really hook the listener, but the multi-tracked guitars give the song a real presence that the rest of the track lacks.

'Back On The Chain' (Campbell/Dee/Kilmister)

Ringing the changes, this is a short story in lyric form that was inspired by American true-crime TV shows, with more than a dash of Bonnie and Clyde on the side. Hints of Bruce Springsteen and Tom Waits show through, but the writer is unique and knows it. The central character is on the run from the police and doesn't want to be sent to prison again.

The musicians provide a choppy backdrop riff that runs through most of the song, except the choruses, and it quickly becomes overly repetitive. The dynamic and somewhat ridiculous solo churns up the song nicely, but, ultimately, the jerky riff becomes stale far too quickly.

'Heroes' (Campbell/Dee/Kilmister)

You could be forgiven for thinking that this will be the old David Bowie chestnut but, ironically, that comes later. Instead, this is another variation on the soldiers in battle theme, with a distinct trenches-of-World-War-I feel to the lyrics. There is an awful couplet that really needed rewriting:

A lot of people dying, men driven raving mad
They scream out there for hours, and it makes you feel really bad

The rest of the lyrics work well here, so this oversight is even more inexplicable. Cameron recalled that Lemmy was less prolific in his writing phase, on this occasion, and was sick for three weeks during the recording, which is the most likely reason.

This mid-tempo plod has all the hallmarks of a lack of inspiration in the tune-writing department as it has little to recommend it. The band seems to be flagging in their composition by this time on the album.

'Time Is Right' (Campbell/Dee/Kilmister)

Seemingly aware that things had slipped, the trio ramp up the pace and throw a sparkling series of riffs together to prove they haven't lost the knack. As well as Phil's nimble fingers on the solo there are also a couple of musical hooks set into the tune. The chorus harmonies are locked in place, which gives the song the lighter tone it requires.

The bleak lyrics are from the point-of-view of a psychopath who revels in pain and torture. It may be a serial killer, it might be the thoughts of a soldier on the battlefield, but either way, it is nihilistic and brutal.

'The Thousand Names Of God' (Campbell/Dee/Kilmister)

Lemmy singled this out as his favourite vocal performance on the album and it is clear to hear why: he injects both real emotion and determination into his expression here. The presence of studio engineer Wesley Mischener on slide guitar is immediately apparent in the opening and he adds an extra dimension to the sonic assault of the tune, recalling the expressive sounds of *Rock 'N' Roll*. The underlying riff is workmanlike and only really comes to life as the song enters its final stages.

The title suggests this is another dose of religion-bashing but the lyrics centre on the stupidity and greed that has led humankind to poison its own environment and yet they praise whichever deity the selfish and venal people of the planet use as a scapegoat. It is a tough note to end on, but the writer was obviously in an angry mood at the time.

Related recordings

'Breaking The Law' (K.K. Downing/Rob Halford/Glenn Tipton)

Motörhead. Recorded: December 2007. Found on: Under Cover (CD)

This is a song that numerous other well-known bands have attempted to cover and, for some reason, the results have always ended in disappointment. Motörhead make a valiant stab at it here, especially as they have Cameron producing, but maybe the song itself is over-rated. The singing invariably sounds flat and the chorus remains weak, even in comparison with the original Judas Priest song, which is far softer than this cranked up, but ultimately mediocre, re-recording.

The problem perhaps stems from the lyrics, which, far from conjuring up a Great Train Robbery, seem to suggest the Keystone Cops have switched sides. Admittedly, the accompanying video for the 1980 song is something of a comedy train wreck (holding up a bank with guitars?!), but surely the song itself is to blame.

'Don't Talk To Me' (Jackie Chambers/Dufort/Kilmister/McAuliffe)

Girlschool. Recorded: June-July 2008. Found on: Legacy (CD)

Such an unexpectedly brilliant song from Girlschool is given an added frisson by the presence of Lemmy, who gets to co-write the lyrics, turn in a fine vocal performance and lend his musical muscle to this gutsy and powerful tune. In a career first, he also gets to play the ...triangle! He chortled long and hard about that.

Lemmy takes the lion's share of the singing, only duetting on the chorus, and adds his unique bass sound to the searing rock on offer. He gels instantly with Denise (who proves a fine replacement for Mikkey) and intertwines with Kim's vocals as if the 'St Valentine's Day Massacre' EP had been recorded yesterday rather than almost thirty years previously. Even the production is up-to-the-minute and in keeping with Motörhead's current output, particularly as it pounds along as if a herd of elephants are charging out of the speakers. You can find this little gem on the album *Legacy* and it deserves a place in your collection.

'Run Rudolph Run' (Chuck Berry)
Lemmy. Recorded: July 2008 . Found on: We Wish You A Metal Xmas And A Headbanging New Year (CD)
There is no other way to say this: it's a bonkers but bizarrely addictive cover of the Chuck Berry warhorse, which comes from a charity album instigated by Ronnie and Wendy Dio.

In case you were wondering, yes, Bob Kulick is at it again with his usual cast of superstars and has-beens, although he manages a surprising coup in the band he assembles around Lemmy: Billy F. Gibbons of ZZ Top lends considerable guitar muscle to this song while Dave Grohl gets to play drums with his hero again. Christmas collections do not come any weirder than this and the sound of Lemmy chewing up the scenery has to be heard to be believed. This is almost beyond criticism, so just lie back and enjoy the outrageous Yuletide nonsense coming out of the speakers.

'Twist and Shout' (Bert Berns/Phil Medley)
Lemmy. Recorded: June 2009. Found on: Harder & Heavier: 60's British Invasion Goes Metal (CD)
Arising from a further Bob Kulick covers collection, this has Lemmy joining Scott Ian (Anthrax) and Greg Bisonnette on another metal shredding of a song most closely associated with The Beatles. The presence of a backing vocalist who sounds like a chipmunk on helium doesn't add to the enjoyment factor (she repeats every single line that Lemmy sings, which becomes annoying after just the second line), but the party atmosphere is compelling and this ultimately ends up on the side of worth-a-listen; just.

'Stand By Me' (Ben King/Jerry Leiber/Mike Stoller)
Lemmy. Recorded: July 2009. Found on: Flip Skateboards: Extremely Sorry (CD)
This frankly bizarre cover of the soul classic (recorded for a skateboard tricks film!), does nothing for the song and doesn't even try to rock it up. The vocals

are bare and untreated (and sound like they were recorded in a shed while Lemmy was waiting for a bus) and the apparent appearance of Dave Lombardo (Slayer) on drums is unfathomable. The drumming is adequate but doesn't show any of the dexterity or power that Dave is famous for. The tune remains, but the struggling vocals, the poor sound and the plodding backbeat leave the song floundering badly. This is one cover version that deserves to be forgotten.

'Paradise Turned Into Dust' (Tim Atkinson/Burston/Steve Clarke/ Kilmister)

Leader Of Down. Recorded: 2009-2010. Found on: Cascade Into Chaos (CD)

Recorded in 2009 for Leader Of Down's debut album, this has a committed lyric and vocal from Lemmy, which he taped in 2010. For many years this album was thought to be lost but, in 2018, Deadline Music (a sub-label of Cleopatra Records) issued *Cascade Into Chaos* with two songs featuring Lemmy. 'Laugh At The Devil 'has already been covered, but this is a brand new track unheard before. There are rumours of a third track, called 'Mr. Wurzel', awaiting release, but information is scant (it may be an early title for this very tune). What is unquestionable is that this is a scorching blast of primal Motörhead for a new generation with a patented Wurzel riff and an overdriven bass sound that reeks of excess. Wurzel plays his heart out and Lemmy gives his all for this affecting goliath of a song. There may be distant echoes, if only thematically, with Joni Mitchell's 'Big Yellow Taxi', but this is carved out of Lemmy's obsessions (politicians, businessmen and soldiers are all covered) and sounds monumental. Worthy of inclusion in any 'best of Lemmy' compilation and, unsurprisingly, boasting the magic touch of Cameron Webb in the mixing.

The World Is Yours (Motörhead Music/UDR/EMI, December 2010)

Personnel:
Lemmy Kilmister: vocals, bass
Phil Campbell: guitars
Mikkey Dee: drums
Produced at NRG, Sage & Sound and Maple Studios, Los Angeles, July-August 2010 by Cameron Webb.
Highest chart place: UK: 45
Running time (approximate): 39:09

While touring the *Motorizer* album in 2009, Mikkey Dee was called up for service on the Swedish version of *I'm A Celebrity, Get Me Out Of Here* and, so, Matt Sorum (ex-Guns 'N' Roses, ex-The Cult, Velvet Revolver, etc.) was contacted and asked to fill in. The story goes that Lemmy texted him saying, 'Matt, I need you to play drums.' To which Matt replied, 'Why me?' and Lemmy sent back the immortal words: 'Dave Grohl's not available.'

Matt maintains it was the most fun he has had on any tour and he was very quick to praise the intricacy and complexity of Mikkey's drumming on the material that he had co-written, acknowledging the sheer physical stamina required to play the songs. Following the tour, Matt remarked: 'I thought either Mikkey would die in the jungle or I would die on the tour!' Mikkey came third and returned to the band soon after.

Mick Green, Lemmy's friend and infrequent collaborator, died in January 2010 at the young age of 61. Lemmy had already had several health scares in the previous few years and had been diagnosed with diabetes in 2000 (the road diet is hardly healthy and nutritious), gastric distress (another symptom of a poor diet) and altitude issues (which meant that travelling had become more uncomfortable for him). He had, remarkably, swapped his signature drink of Jack Daniels and coke for the 'healthier' Vodka and orange juice around 2009. In later years Lemmy was heard to utter a caution to other musicians: 'I think this rock 'n' roll business might be bad for the human life.'

'Born To Lose' (Campbell/Dee/Kilmister)

Mikkey gives a brief introductory drum workout and then the whole song explodes into life with a staggering and inspired hook-laden riff. Phil sounds like he is channelling Eddie and has come up with one of the few corkers that Eddie missed. Inevitably this has modern production values attached to it, so it is both heavier and clearer, but this is undoubtedly a sparkling throwback to the early years. The vocal melody verges on the periphery of nostalgia, suggesting songs from 1979 (although Lemmy's voice is weaker and certainly has the odd slur), while the lyrics seem to pander to that idea by resurrecting an early motto and finally naming a song after it.

This is not mere sentimentality for past times but a vital piece of the current band acknowledging their heritage and illustrating how they can still pull a winner out of the bag, even this late into their career.

'I Know How To Die' (Campbell/Dee/Kilmister)

Opting for a disguised rock and roll riff, this continues the unexpected quality of the opener, although Chuck Berry never heard a guitar quite like this. There is room for piano accompaniment on the choruses, but the option is never explored, probably because the band was already happy with it.

Mortality seems to be on the lyricist's mind and, given recent diagnoses and periods of illness, this is not a shock. This is a bullish restatement that Lemmy will live his life exactly as he pleases and that is how legends are born.

'Get Back In Line' (Campbell/Dee/Kilmister)

Mulling over the conundrum that the meek are supposed to inherit the Earth, the lyrics explore the real-world chances of that happening. It is summed up with the last lines of the three verses:

... All things come to he who waits, the waiting never ends ...
... All things come to he who waits but these days most things suck ...
... All things come to he who waits, but all things come too late ...

The tune has a rock and roll sensibility while keeping the melody light, although Mikkey's percussion use is both repetitive and too high in the mix. It is a rare example of a misstep from a consummate drummer.

'Devils In My Head' (Campbell/Dee/Kilmister)

With the title harking back to 1993's 'Devils' one could be forgiven for thinking that was simply a variation on a theme. Not a bit of it, there is no hint of psychedelia in the tune and the words are certainly harsher in tone. Lemmy's vocals are grittier and the slurring is more pronounced and occurs throughout the chorus, which suggests this is a conscious decision rather than a sign of accident or ageing.

The lyrics are impressive but world-weary and resigned, word paintings without any obvious comedic content (that is reserved for the booklet illustrations from Lemmy, which rather highlight his delight at simple puns and sight gags). As an album track, this passes muster, but it is a step down from the opening salvo of songs.

'Rock 'n' Roll Music' (Campbell/Dee/Kilmister)

A simple love song to his musical life, this has a lyric that compares favourably with the ancient 'Rock 'N' Roll'; the music actually has a thrusting momentum (and an eerily familiar opening riff) which is entirely undercut when the song is diverted into the actual tune which is formulaic rock and roll that Chuck Berry *would* recognise. The vocals, especially the harmonies and the chorus, have an earworm catchiness to them that make up for the limp central riff, but they can't pull the song completely out of the mire.

'Waiting For The Snake' (Campbell/Dee/Kilmister)
There is a distinct heavy metal gloss to the riff that comes tearing out of the speakers here and it carries the song through the mood changes that follow. The solo plays up to the same aesthetic and it is only the lack of a killer chorus or a memorable vocal melody that keeps this monster riff from escaping.

The words are apocalyptic and the metaphor of the snake clearly refers to Satan and the Earth's Armageddon. Perhaps Lemmy had just been reading the book of Revelations because he undoubtedly sees the end of the human race and a wholesale move to Hell for the planet's inhabitants.

'Brotherhood Of Man' (Campbell/Dee/Kilmister)
Bill Ward, Black Sabbath's founding drummer, has said that he plays this song frequently on his radio show because 'it seems quite fitting in today's society'. What he is referring to is the pessimistic outlook put forward by the words and the deeply sarcastic title.

Over a bastardised 'Orgasmatron' riff (and parts of the vocal melody from the same source) cataclysmic words carry on the ragingly bleak tone of the album so far.

Lemmy and Phil both get brooding solos which simply add to the gloomy atmosphere. The song is memorable and accomplished, but the undoubted echoes of its predecessor cast a long and heavy shadow.

'Outlaw' (Campbell/Dee/Kilmister)
Lemmy rarely found it hard to write lyrics, but he did have a few tricks that he used. Writing opposites was one and here we have an example: 'Lawman' from 1979 becomes 'Outlaw' here. Taking the same Cowboy inspiration that served him so well with Eddie, he pens a Western just in time for the inevitable gunfight.

The band joins him in a Metallica-esque romp that features a remarkable chorus vocal where the singer appears to be gargling razor blades while the backing vocals dive in and out in a unique addition to the Motörhead sound.

This is a complex number that requires precision timing and some great dexterity and it is a fantastic achievement that combines old and new in one savage tune.

'I Know What You Need' (Campbell/Dee/Kilmister)
Singing about escape, paranoia and violent death in a voice on the edge of hysteria or insanity embellishes the basic thrust of the lyrics and sits rather well with the almost jump blues riff that characterises the song.

Throwing in a riff-based break and then expanding it into another treble-heavy guitar solo (while Mikkey ranges around the kit) is a striking manoeuvre from Phil, which adds a great deal to the impact of the tune.

'Bye Bye Bitch Bye Bye' (Campbell/Dee/Kilmister)

No one can deny Lemmy's unreconstructed lyrics here, even if they are a fantasy revenge penned when he apparently broke up with his long-term girlfriend. It's a rather brutal kiss-off to a cheating partner, although the irony of Lemmy writing these words does not go unnoticed.

The band finish the album with a rough-house rock and roll tune that stinks of déjà vu but manages to carry off the track with a mixture of brio and bravura playing that raises a smile even if the words are somewhat venomous. The closing solo has a brashness to it that cannot be ignored.

Related recordings

'Doctor Alibi' (Saul Hudson/Kilmister)

Slash. Recorded: January 2010. Found on: Slash (CD)

The final part of the Doctor trilogy is a startlingly autobiographical contribution to the debut solo album by Slash, who enlisted a variety of guest vocalists to adorn his assured musicianship. Lemmy writes of the candid warning from his doctor, that the life he was leading would soon kill him if he carried on this way. The bulk of the lyrics are a denial that anything is wrong and a justification for his continued ill-treatment of his body. As noted previously, Lemmy had had several health scares and was diagnosed with at least two lifelong conditions (gastric issues and diabetes) that would shorten his life. Lemmy summed up his smoking and drinking lifestyle by saying he continued with 'dogged insolence in the face of mounting opposition to the contrary'.

Slash is undoubtedly unique in his tone and approach; the sound he achieves is instantly identifiable. The tune he provides here has an old school hard rock and roll panache, buttressed by galumphing drums, which suits the urgency of the vocals and there is even a bit of signature bass work visible on this cracking song.

The HeadCat - Walk The Walk...Talk The Talk (Niji Entertainment, July 2011)

Personnel:
Lemmy Kilmister: vocals, bass
Slim Jim Phantom: drums
Danny B Harvey: guitars, piano
T J McDonnell: percussion
Produced at Sage and Sound Studios, Hollywood, June 2010 by Cameron Webb.
Highest chart place: Did not chart
Running time (approximate): 27:36

Having had such a great time on their first effort, Lemmy, Slim and Danny finally found the time to record a second Head Cat album. It was taped quickly, just before *The World Is Yours*, but with the same team behind the desk and at the same studio. Impressively, there was still enough time for the Head Cat to compose two songs while they were rehearsing. Niji Entertainment, the record label the band eventually signed to, was owned and run by Lemmy's great friends Ronnie and Wendy Dio.

In order that the Head Cat album was not lost in the wake of a new Motörhead disc, it was held back for over a year and, in a piece of unhappy cosmic irony, Wurzel died the same month that the album actually came out: July 2011.

'American Beat' (Danny B Harvey/Kilmister/Slim Jim Phantom)

Sticking a drum-led band composition at the start of the album is a brave move but, boy, does it work. Returning to his natural instrument, Lemmy produces a fine bass racket for this newly forged song. Bubbling with the sheer excitement of creating new rock and roll gives the tune a sense of fun and enjoyment.

Keeping it short and sharp (well, the original rock and roll bands only had two minutes to play with on early singles) The Head Cat announce their presence, drop a strapping opening song into the ether and leave. They could have been huge if they had been able to capitalise on the hook-driven material they were producing. Motörhead, it transpired, were the wife while the Head Cat was only the intermittent girlfriend. Lemmy sings with passion and attempts to sum up his love of rock and roll with a nostalgic but urgent lyric.

'Say Mama' (Johnny Earl/Joe Meek)

A ripe rockabilly treat, with a repetitive piano riff, this is injected with a hint of steel from the production and a modicum of light-heartedness with the 'wo-wo' accompaniment on the chorus. The crucial element here is that the trio are obviously enjoying themselves while Lemmy takes his foot off the pedal and eases back into his favourite era of music. The original single was released by Gene Vincent in 1958.

'I Ain't Never' (Webb Pierce/Mel Tillis)

Born of two country music artists co-writing the song, the first version was put out in 1959. The Head Cat beef up the rockabilly arrangement slightly but carry the country vibe through to the finished track. Lemmy double-tracks his croon (!) and, sweetly, carries the tune off with aplomb.

'Bad Boy' (Larry Williams)

A failed single by the writer, in 1958, this tune was resurrected by The Beatles in 1965 and only initially released in America. The trio here opts for the Fab Four's arrangement, although the aged vocals from Lemmy rather flatten the rebellious teenage spirit of the song. The Head Cat provide a perfect backing and the net result is a tidy little track that doesn't outstay its welcome.

'Shakin' All Over' (Heath)

This is a Johnny Kidd and the Pirates original from 1960, which was a number one hit in the U.K. It was a huge favourite of Lemmy's and inspired his lifelong love affair with rock and roll. He was paying homage to his heroes (as he had on previous occasions) and he produced a rawer and more nuanced vocal than might have been expected. Danny continues to shine with his spot-on guitar work and recreated solos, while Slim shows how effortless drumming standing up can appear to be.

'Let It Rock' (Chuck Berry)

Along with Little Richard (strangely under-represented in Head Cat recordings), Chuck Berry is at the forefront of rock and roll. This 1960 song has a distinct 'Roll Over Beethoven'/'Johnny B. Goode' riff powering its rock and roll heart and it ends up sounding a little second-hand in comparison to its predecessors. Nevertheless, the band attack the song with vigour and acquit themselves honourably.

'Something Else' (Robert Cochran/Sharon Seeley)

There is a particular vocal required for this vintage 1959 Eddie Cochran tune that Lemmy nails with ease, probably because it concerns a nervous young man trying to impress a girl with an out-of-his-budget car. The first-person lyrics lend immediacy to the song, as does the lascivious singing.

The song was written by Eddie's older brother and Eddie's girlfriend at the time. Eddie died in 1960 while touring the U.K. and the Head Cat pay suitable homage on this sterling cover.

'The Eagle Flies on Friday' (Harvey/Kilmister/Phantom)

Again self-penned, this has Motörhead stamped in its genes, although its pace is more horse and cart than thundering locomotive. The plodding 'chuck-a-chuck-a' rhythm guitar suggests many early rock and roll numbers and a definite blues influence, but it careens into a heavy middle eight that carries on until the song ends, along with the blues-rock solo that interjects every so often.

Lemmy slips in a nice little lyric, talking again about how there are just:

Two kinds of people in the world
You know, one holds out a helping hand
And the other will screw you in the dirt

... which is as accurate a summation of his philosophy as could be wished for.

'Trying To Get To You' (Rose Marie McCoy/Charles Singleton)

A 1954 song, made famous by Elvis Presley in 1956, which gets a rockabilly trundle from the Head Cat. Lemmy again proves up to the vocal task, which is harder than it sounds as there is a distinct lack of breathing space between certain lines, while Danny releases his inner Scotty Moore in the guitar breaks. Slim keeps a remarkably steady beat and props up the lower registers nicely, Lemmy having his bass set to full treble here.

'You Can't Do That' (Lennon/McCartney)

The Head Cat were huge Beatles fans and this 1964 deep catalogue tune barely needed a rehearsal given their encyclopaedic knowledge of the band. The version presented here is pretty similar to that first release, complete with harmony and softened backing vocals from Lemmy that highlight his rather tuneful singing voice. It is not one of the Beatles' best, but it has a sturdy hook and a staccato tune that appeal.

'It'll Be Me' (Jack Clement)

This is a popular choice of cover for hard rock bands as Deep Purple also recorded their version of this 1957 Jerry Lee Lewis corker for their successful *Now What?!* album in 2013. They won't have appropriated the arrangement from this Head Cat recording, however, as this is very similar to the original. Lemmy sings with real glee and the solos are pure rock and roll; Danny also spraying piano all over this short and sweet stormer.

'Crossroads' (Robert Johnson)

An antique blues number from the dawn of recorded music, this 1936 song was titled 'Cross Road Blues' by its author, but it was raised like Lazarus by Eric Clapton for Cream's 1966 album *Fresh Cream*, which created an electric guitar-led blues-rock monster that influenced future versions of the song for decades to come. That includes this Head Cat recording, although the guitar soloing is shortened and notable for its mutation into a far more recognisable rock and roll solo. It is a surprising musical sidestep for the group, but it does update this veteran tune nicely and gives it an unexpected new lease of life for the twenty-first century.

Related recording

'It Still Hurts' (Andreas Bruhn/Doro Pesch)

Doro. Recorded: March 2012. Found on: Raise Your Fist (CD)

Doro immediately saw this song as a chance to duet with Lemmy again and sent the track over for him to record his vocals in his home town. She would not know it, but this was her last opportunity to collaborate with her friend. He recorded his parts in March 2012, remarking at the time that it was just another fun track to work on. Lemmy was presented with a virtually complete backing track and sang his evocative vocals, intertwining with Doro's guide presence on this mournful rock ballad. The melancholic mood seems like premonition, but both singers give great performances, Lemmy moving outside of his comfort zone to produce an emotive and frail-voiced reading.

Aftershock (Motörhead Music/UDR, October 2013)

Personnel:
Lemmy Kilmister: vocals, bass
Phil Campbell: guitars, piano
Mikkey Dee: drums
Produced at NRG, Sound Factory, Sunset Sound and Maple Studios, Los Angeles, January 2013 by Cameron Webb.
Highest chart place: UK: 110
Running time (approximate): 46:54

When Motörhead finally reconvened to record a new album, there was a distinct sense of loss in the air following the deaths of John Entwistle, Mick Green, Wurzel and Ronnie James Dio, to name just a few.

'Heartbreaker' (Campbell/Dee/Kilmister)

Not a cover of the aching Led Zeppelin song, this is a bleakly despairing rant about the folly of conflict and the dehumanisation that results. Lyrically, Lemmy seems to be on fire, raging through his words:

> You remember what you said in the first attack
> Stand your ground, fight your best, drop them in their tracks
> Now the story changed again, sing a different song
> Listen how the shots ring out, on and on and on

There is even space for a nod at Hawkwind in the passing lyric 'monsters at the edge of time', but this is hardly a light-hearted reference.
Mikkey and Phil provide a stampeding backing to the verses and the chorus is curiously catchy in its simplicity (Lemmy takes the vocals up a musical notch while opting not to back it up with harmonies). This short sharp statement is the first in an album full of pithy songs.

'Coup De Grace' (Campbell/Dee/Kilmister)

Always ready for rock and roll playtime, there's a joy to this tune that is undercut by the cynical words. The vocal melody is again lighter for the chorus and the relative speed of this track gives it a defiantly modern feel.
The singing is characterised by the undoubted slurring that has crept into the voice. This is not just an affectation for this song, however, but a sign of an ongoing deterioration. Oddly, this has the effect of lightening the vocals, at times and allowing more melodic hooks to show through.

'Lost Woman Blues' (Campbell/Dee/Kilmister)

A blues-rock groove slows the pace of the album without losing the listener.
A regretful song, clearly inspired by the initial blues tune, this speeds up into

149

an Eddie-era stomp for the remainder of the song. The world-weariness of the lyrics is matched by the carefully constructed music.

'End Of Time' (Campbell/Dee/Kilmister)
Ruminating on the present day, although using the literary device of distancing by suggesting that the author is looking back at the past from his perspective at the end of the world, the narrator sees a depressingly bleak future ahead for the human race.

Placing these thoughts over a punked-up pace and a cutting yet catchy riff is a masterstroke that captures the band at their virile best, still able to write hook-laden songs that show they are able to leave their compatriots watching in wonder.

'Do You Believe' (Campbell/Dee/Kilmister)
The simple rock and roll riff that opens this song doesn't prepare the listener for the thundering onslaught that transpires. Adding a touch of comedy in the lyrics (referring to someone as 'Hell on roller skates' raises a smile) is indisputably in response to the amusing dance/shuffle beat that occupies the middle eight. The solos section that finishes the song is perhaps overdone but the sense of fun around this tune is infectious.

'Death Machine' (Campbell/Dee/Kilmister)
Back to the desolation and starkness of mortality (the previous glimpse of humour now gone) with an arid lyric about total warfare and a chillingly bare musical backing which has an early Black Sabbath feel to the main riff, albeit at a quicker tempo. The chorus is barely distinguishable from the verses; it is the musical changes that provide an instrumental chorus of sorts. This feels more like a complex demo arrangement that needed the producer to pummel it into a more coherent shape.

'Dust And Glass' (Campbell/Dee/Kilmister)
There is a despairing mood to the lyrics, which look like a tone poem that was then set to music, which complements the down-tuned blues backing. The bass is the lead melodic instrument until the solo scythes in. In another short song, it is noteworthy that an acoustic guitar was deemed unnecessary as the bass nicely fills the sonic space.

'Going To Mexico' (Campbell/Dee/Kilmister)
Anyone who thinks this is 'Going To Brazil' rewritten is in for a shock. The words concern criminals making for the border and the non-extradition status of Mexico, where you won't have to serve any prison time.

The music has a stupidly blunt riff bastardised from 'Ace of Spades' and features some blisteringly complicated drum work from Mikkey just to increase the musicianship quota. There are echoes of previous songs visible, but the sheer attack of the tune wipes out any hint of self-plagiarism.

'Silence When You Speak To Me' (Campbell/Dee/Kilmister)
Utilising a grinding riff that has the weight of an advancing tank, this is another despairing look at the human condition. Phil provides a brutal but appealing solo and the chorus has a surprising ability to capture the imagination despite the churning undercarriage and the serious lyrics.

Whatever took hold of the band when they were writing this album, it has resulted in this prolific vomit of songs that share a despondent atmosphere.

'Crying Shame' (Campbell/Dee/Kilmister)
Amphetamine-fuelled rock and roll never sounded quite as brutal as it does here. The hammered piano on the chorus is a nice touch, but it doesn't disguise the misogynistic flavour of the lyrics or the pervading gloom of the music.

Although not one of their finest songs, the audacity and brass neck of the lyrics allow the tune to lurk memorably in the subconscious.

'Queen Of The Damned' (Campbell/Dee/Kilmister)
Anne Rice has written a series of vampire books, starting with *Interview with the Vampire*, the third of which is titled *Queen of the Damned*. Given the lyrical thrust of the song, roughly summed up as 'get out of town, or she will eviscerate you', it is certainly possible that Lemmy gained some inspiration from this work (especially as it was made into a farcical B movie where the vampire Lestat becomes a hard rock star: someone will have watched this in the tour bus while travelling).

Lemmy gives it maximum treble and maximum distortion on his bass opening, which actually creates a real bass-shaped hole in the sound, which Phil barely tries to cover, while Mikkey throws in the towel and just concentrates on double footwork and speed to imitate the sonic architecture of punk.

'Knife' (Campbell/Dee/Kilmister)
An unexpected allusion to the plague of knife crime that came to the fore in the U.K., this has Lemmy musing on the use of knives in the desert, snakes and the inevitability of death. Phil layers on a series of almost subliminal riffs, the most prominent of which does a nice line in melody, although the solo proves banal and the over-used riff becomes annoying by the end.

'Keep Your Powder Dry' (Campbell/Dee/Kilmister)
Using the title as a metaphor for a rallying cry (i.e. make sure you are ready for conflict), Lemmy unpacks the age-old phrase that summons up images of ships' cannons and early flintlock pistols and the need to ensure gunpowder remained dry. This advice was credited to Oliver Cromwell in 1856 as he waged

a campaign in Ireland. However, the maxim was first noted in an 1834 poem, 'Oliver's Advice' by William Blacker, where the sentence 'put your trust in God, my boys, and keep your powder dry' initially appeared in the Dublin University Magazine.

The almost slobbered vocal sits on top of an AC/DC riff from Phil that could have graced *Rock Or Bust* without comment. In keeping with that pedigree, this has the most ebullient feel of all the tracks on this album.

'Paralyzed' (Campbell/Dee/Kilmister)

To end proceedings on a high, Phil pulls out a stentorian riff while Mikkey thrashes his kit with precision, recalling Philthy at his heaviest, and Lemmy sings the nonsense words as if they were Shakespeare on acid. It is a storming finale to a remarkably assured album and, aside from the slurred delivery, shows the band are completely in command of their musical destiny.

Related recording

'Rock City' (Richard Z. Kruspe)

Emigrate. Recorded: July 2014. Found on: Silent So Long (CD)

Emigrate are the alternative metal solo project of Rammstein's lead guitarist. There's a galloping drum introduction that leads straight into the meat of the riff and Lemmy speak-sings the verses before he captures the higher ground with a sturdy chorus that elevates this to essential listening, even with the synthesizers and keyboards beefing up the soundscape. The vocals are mixed just a little too low, although that was obviously the intention. Despite the lack of any musical or lyrical involvement from Lemmy, this is a quintessential collaboration.

While it is tempting to contemplate, this song was not inspired by Nottingham's Rock City nightclub and venue!

Bad Magic (Motörhead Music/UDR, August 2015)

Personnel:
Lemmy Kilmister: vocals, bass
Phil Campbell: guitars, piano
Mikkey Dee: drums
Brian May: guitar visitation on 'The Devil'
Produced at NRG, Grandmaster and Maple Studios, Los Angeles, April-May 2015 by Cameron Webb.
Highest chart place: UK: 10
Running time (approximate): 42:57

The death of Motörhead's long-time roadie Dave 'Hobbs' Hilsden (he covered several jobs in his decades-long attachment to the band) following *Aftershock* came as a shattering blow to the already long list of close friends and acquaintances who died after that album's release: Tommy Ramone, Jack Bruce, Phil Everly, Alvin Stardust and Johnny Winter among them. Lemmy was showing his age in both his live appearances (where he used a walking stick to come on stage) and in his vocals. On top of his diabetes, he appeared to be a frail figure when the band were touring.

Nevertheless, the band soldiered on. In a marked change to established practice, they wrote around five of the songs while they were in the studio to ensure the spontaneity remained.

Bad Magic is a timeless summation of all that is great about Motörhead. It has the authentic stamp of legacy about it and it is a remarkable if accidental, swan song that provides a fittingly Devil-may-care end to an undeniably extraordinary career.

Motörhead are a legend and their name will live on. Lemmy, in his turn, has become an icon, the last true rock and roll hero.

'Victory Or Die' (Campbell/Dee/Kilmister)

Greeted with a bracing tune and a packed set of lyrics, the opening to the 40th-anniversary album has all the hallmarks of a valedictory run. The trio know what they are doing and they do it well. The only sign that they aren't bulletproof is the lack of a chorus hook, which is left to the music to provide instead. Lemmy sounds feral but aged here, the deterioration in the voice audible from the previous album.

'Thunder & Lightning' (Campbell/Dee/Kilmister)

Mikkey, on the other hand, is as vital and punchy as ever and continues to show the sheer power and control he has over his instrument.

Speeding along like men half their age, this is a song about the joy of touring and the excitement of being on stage. This has the distinct feel of a written-in-the-studio track as Phil throws in a wild solo that sounds spontaneous. The surprise here is that, in his 69th year, Lemmy continues to play at punk velocity and sing with studied vigour.

'Fire Storm Hotel' (Campbell/Dee/Kilmister)

The words conjure images of arson and murder while the music lopes around with an Eddie-style riff and a rock and roll chassis. The chorus has a nice hook and the tune doesn't outstay its welcome. The band appears to have hit a songwriting groove that shows no sign of letting up.

'Shoot Out All Your Lights' (Campbell/Dee/Kilmister)

Mikkey's drum track is given pride of place at the start of this energetic and punishing tune. The guitar riffs collide with each other while Lemmy urges his bass on for the squealing solo. There is such a sense of urgency and enjoyment in these songs, it suggests that even old troopers like Motörhead can get a second wind and come up with great music.

'The Devil' (Campbell/Dee/Kilmister)

After a reversed guitar entry, the piledriver rhythm establishes itself briefly before the faster verse riff comes into play. The chorus reverts to the catchy pounding beat of the opening and then, for the solo, Queen's Brian May drops in for a 'visitation'(as the sleeve notes have it). The solo fits nicely (and Phil could have come up with something similar), but it is the tone of Brian's home-built guitar that is unique.

Using that old heavy metal stand-by, Lucifer, is not remotely original, but the words are less important than the music, particularly at this point in their career.

'Electricity' (Campbell/Dee/Kilmister)

While the lyrics skirt around the subject (playing rock and roll is good for the soul), the tune hammers the point home with a deliberately fourth-hand punk riff battered into the shape of a song. Phil gets to strangle his guitar on the solo and the chorus is melodic and barmy in equal measure. As a tip of the hat to Ramones and The Damned, it is a sparky little ditty that delights in its own brevity.

'Evil Eye' (Campbell/Dee/Kilmister)

The nearest thing to a title track is this paranoid tale of curses and black magic. It has a rolling tribal beat and a peculiar whispered and growled chorus, which, while trying to reflect the intensity of the words, loses any sense of the tune. The verses promise a lot, but the flat chorus really lets the song down despite sterling support from Phil and Mikkey.

'Teach Them How To Bleed' (Campbell/Dee/Kilmister)

Recycling an old Wurzel riff on the bass, Lemmy attacks this tune with venom and sets a ferocious pace for his bandmates. Phil seems to have solo-itis as he jams in guitar breaks wherever he can and they only add to the spirit of this self-homage. The inevitable slowed-down rock and roll ending adds to the feeling of farewell that haunts this album, even in the lyrics:

It's the final act now
Time for us to leave
Eat the sun, eat the gun
Teach them how to bleed

Mortality was on everyone's mind, it seemed.

'Till The End' (Campbell/Dee/Kilmister)
This is where Lemmy becomes truly contemplative and autobiographical. Imagine you are sitting next to him in a bar and listening to his thoughts about life and how he has lived it. It is unrepentant in tone but entirely comfortable in feeling. If this hadn't been the last album, lyrically, Lemmy would have had nowhere to go next time.

The music is a slow-burning country blues-based ballad, only played on electric instruments, and the chorus enhances the ruminative mood with the audible vocal strain. Sounding loose and extemporised, this is another example of the studio-written songs that pepper this album.

'Tell Me Who To Kill' (Campbell/Dee/Kilmister)
Phil rips out a real metal riff and then passes the torch to Lemmy, who carries the riff on his treble-heavy bass and instantly turns the tune into a Motörhead cracker. The song pulsates with passion and commitment, although the words are a little impenetrable, and both the guitar and bass share the solo spot: the fingerwork from the bass player is remarkable both for its dexterity and strength.

'Choking On Your Screams' (Campbell/Dee/Kilmister)
Uniquely, this is a full-blooded alien invasion story from the usually grounded Lemmy. It postulates a warrior people far stronger than the human race and it details the devastation and destruction visited upon the Earth. There is great glee in the vocals when they are singing the title, but it is the music that astounds: drawkcab guitars and vocals imitate rough synthesizers while Phil pulls a grinding Dave Brock riff from his pocket, which merges seamlessly with the treacle pace. The arrangement and solo are entirely Motörhead, but the Hawkwind echoes are apparent throughout, even when the chorus speeds up and the vocals enter a gargled 'Orgasmatron' realm. Talk about revisiting the past.

'When The Sky Comes Looking For You' (Campbell/Dee/Kilmister)
Counter-pointing that with this ferocious but celebratory tune as the final self-composed song is a masterstroke. The trio show off their undoubted

instrumental skills on a barnstorming track that has a groove that will get even the grumpiest of audience members on their feet and baltering about with abandon.

It is a stirring end to an album that acknowledges the past but illustrates how relevant the band still was. We shall not see their like again.

'Sympathy For The Devil' (Jagger/Richards)
Think of this as a bonus track to the core album. Triple H requested that they do this cover and they duly obliged, but the limitations in the vocals and the rearrangement are plain to hear, even though they put all their love and sweat and beers into the recording. Lemmy chews the words with panache while Phil sprays some overwrought soloing into the pot. Mikkeygives a good account of himself but lacks the laid-back jazz simplicity of Charlie Watts, which characterised the original recording.

Related recording
'Heroes' (David Bowie/Brian Eno)
Motörhead. Recorded: May 2015 Found on: Under Cover (CD)
The instigator of this impressive toughened up cover was Phil, who badgered Lemmy to cut this version before the moment passed altogether. Once it had been recorded, Lemmy was vocal in his pride at the way it had turned out. Even the Robert Fripp guitar lines that float over the song were reproduced. Lemmy brought his own idiosyncratic singing style to the event, but it blends well with the heavier backing. This is a surprisingly successful cover which makes it a pity that the oft-contemplated covers album from Motörhead never really materialised.

David Bowie himself died on January 10th 2016, aged only 69. In November 2015, Philthy had unexpectedly died, aged just 61. Heroes were disappearing at an alarming rate.

The End

Following the release of the album, Motörhead inevitably headed out on tour. It was clear that Lemmy was continuing to find live appearances draining both physically and mentally, he was hospitalised for a lung infection in September but bounced back enough to return to the road to complete the first round of touring on December 11th 2015, commemorated on the live album *Clean Your Clock*, and Lemmy returned to his home in L.A. to celebrate his forthcoming 70th birthday and the attendant Christmas.

After a big birthday bash in the week before Christmas, manager Todd Singerman noted that Lemmy was looking very unwell and he was hospitalised immediately. After a brain scan, Lemmy was released and returned to his apartment. The results came through a couple of days later and they showed cancer in his brain and his neck. It was clearly terminal.

Managing to make his 70th birthday, and even seeing out Christmas, Lemmy died on 28 December from prostate cancer, cardiac arrhythmia and, ultimately, congestive heart failure. It was the end to a remarkable life, lived as Lemmy had desired, independent and on his own terms. His legacy will undoubtedly make him immortal.

Alive, Lemmy was a legend, in death, he is mythic. The last true rock and roller has left the building.

On Track series

Tori Amos – Lisa Torem 978-1-78952-142-9

Asia – Peter Braidis 978-1-78952-099-6

Barclay James Harvest – Keith and Monica Domone 978-1-78952-067-5

The Beatles – Andrew Wild 978-1-78952-009-5

The Beatles Solo 1969-1980 – Andrew Wild 978-1-78952-030-9

Blue Oyster Cult – Jacob Holm-Lupo 978-1-78952-007-1

Marc Bolan and T.Rex – Peter Gallagher 978-1-78952-124-5

Kate Bush – Bill Thomas 978-1-78952-097-2

Camel – Hamish Kuzminski 978-1-78952-040-8

Caravan – Andy Boot 978-1-78952-127-6

Eric Clapton Solo – Andrew Wild 978-1-78952-141-2

The Clash – Nick Assirati 978-1-78952-077-4

Crosby, Stills and Nash – Andrew Wild 978-1-78952-039-2

The Damned – Morgan Brown 978-1-78952-136-8

Deep Purple and Rainbow 1968-79 – Steve Pilkington 978-1-78952-002-6

Dire Straits – Andrew Wild 978-1-78952-044-6

The Doors – Tony Thompson 978-1-78952-137-5

Dream Theater – Jordan Blum 978-1-78952-050-7

Elvis Costello and The Attractions – Georg Purvis 978-1-78952-129-0

Emerson Lake and Palmer – Mike Goode 978-1-78952-000-2

Fairport Convention – Kevan Furbank 978-1-78952-051-4

Peter Gabriel – Graeme Scarfe 978-1-78952-138-2

Genesis – Stuart MacFarlane 978-1-78952-005-7

Gentle Giant – Gary Steel 978-1-78952-058-3

Gong – Kevan Furbank 978-1-78952-082-8

Hawkwind – Duncan Harris 978-1-78952-052-1

Roy Harper – Opher Goodwin 978-1-78952-130-6

Iron Maiden – Steve Pilkington 978-1-78952-061-3

Jethro Tull – Jordan Blum 978-1-78952-016-3

Elton John in the 1970s – Peter Kearns 978-1-78952-034-7

Gong – Kevan Furbank 978-1-78952-082-8

The Incredible String Band – Tim Moon 978-1-78952-107-8

Iron Maiden – Steve Pilkington 978-1-78952-061-3

Judas Priest – John Tucker 978-1-78952-018-7

Kansas – Kevin Cummings 978-1-78952-057-6

Level 42 – Matt Philips 978-1-78952-102-3

Aimee Mann – Jez Rowden 978-1-78952-036-1

Joni Mitchell – Peter Kearns 978-1-78952-081-1

The Moody Blues – Geoffrey Feakes 978-1-78952-042-2

Mike Oldfield – Ryan Yard 978-1-78952-060-6

Tom Petty – Richard James 978-1-78952-128-3

Queen – Andrew Wild 978-1-78952-003-3

Renaissance – David Detmer 978-1-78952-062-0

The Rolling Stones 1963-80 – Steve Pilkington 978-1-78952-017-0
Steely Dan – Jez Rowden 978-1-78952-043-9
Steve Hackett – Geoffrey Feakes 978-1-78952-098-9
Thin Lizzy – Graeme Stroud 978-1-78952-064-4
Toto – Jacob Holm-Lupo 978-1-78952-019-4
U2 – Eoghan Lyng 978-1-78952-078-1
UFO – Richard James 978-1-78952-073-6
The Who – Geoffrey Feakes 978-1-78952-076-7
Roy Wood and the Move – James R Turner 978-1-78952-008-8
Van Der Graaf Generator – Dan Coffey 978-1-78952-031-6
Yes – Stephen Lambe 978-1-78952-001-9
Frank Zappa 1966 to 1979 – Eric Benac 978-1-78952-033-0
10CC – Peter Kearns 978-1-78952-054-5

Decades Series

Alice Cooper in the 1970s – Chris Sutton 978-1-78952-104-7
Curved Air in the 1970s – Laura Shenton 978-1-78952-069-9
Fleetwood Mac in the 1970s – Andrew Wild 978-1-78952-105-4
Focus in the 1970s – Stephen Lambe 978-1-78952-079-8
Marillion in the 1980s – Nathaniel Webb 978-1-78952-065-1
Pink Floyd In The 1970s – Georg Purvis 978-1-78952-072-9
The Sweet in the 1970s – Darren Johnson 978-1-78952-139-9
Uriah Heep in the 1970s – Steve Pilkington 978-1-78952-103-0

On Screen series

Carry On... – Stephen Lambe 978-1-78952-004-0
David Cronenberg – Patrick Chapman 978-1-78952-071-2
Doctor Who: The David Tennant Years – Jamie Hailstone 978-1-78952-066-8
Monty Python – Steve Pilkington 978-1-78952-047-7
Seinfeld Seasons 1 to 5 – Stephen Lambe 978-1-78952-012-5

Other Books

Babysitting A Band On The Rocks – G.D. Praetorius 978-1-78952-106-1
Derek Taylor: For Your Radioactive Children – Andrew Darlington 978-1-78952-038-5
Iggy and The Stooges On Stage 1967-1974 – Per Nilsen 978-1-78952-101-6
Jon Anderson and the Warriors – the road to Yes – David Watkinson 978-1-78952-059-0
Nu Metal: A Definitive Guide – Matt Karpe 978-1-78952-063-7
Tommy Bolin: In and Out of Deep Purple – Laura Shenton 978-1-78952-070-5
Maximum Darkness – Deke Leonard 978-1-78952-048-4
Maybe I Should've Stayed In Bed – Deke Leonard 978-1-78952-053-8
The Twang Dynasty – Deke Leonard 978-1-78952-049-1

and many more to come!

Would you like to write for Sonicbond Publishing?
We are mainly a music publisher, but we also occasionally
publish in other genres including film and television. At Sonicbond
Publishing we are always on the look-out for authors, particularly for
our two main series, On Track and Decades.

Mixing fact with in depth analysis, the On Track series examines
the entire recorded work of a particular musical artist or group. All
genres are considered from easy listening and jazz to 60s soul to 90s
pop, via rock and metal.

The Decades series singles out a particular decade in an artist or
group's history and focuses on that decade in more detail than may
be allowed in the On Track series.

While professional writing experience would, of course, be
an advantage, the most important qualification is to have real
enthusiasm and knowledge of your subject. First-time authors are
welcomed, but the ability to write well in English is essential.

Sonicbond Publishing has distribution throughout Europe and
North America, and all our books are also published in E-book form.
Authors will be paid a royalty based on sales of their book.
Further details about our books are available from
www.sonicbondpublishing.com. To contact us, complete the
contact form there or email info@sonicbondpublishing.co.uk